D0297077

992335485 7
WITHDRAWN

Stonework

Weekend DIY

Stonework

15 step-by-step projects

Quick and easy ideas to enhance your garden

Alan & Gill Bridgewater

NEW
HOLLAND

First published in 2003 by New Holland Publishers (UK) Ltd
London • Cape Town • Sydney • Auckland

Garfield House, 86–88 Edgware Road, London W2 2EA, United Kingdom
www.newhollandpublishers.com

80 McKenzie Street, Cape Town 8001, South Africa

Level 1, Unit 4, 14 Aquatic Drive, Frenchs Forest, NSW 2086, Australia

218 Lake Road, Northcote, Auckland

Copyright © 2003 text New Holland Publishers (UK) Ltd
Copyright © 2003 illustrations and photographs New Holland Publishers (UK) Ltd
Copyright © 2003 New Holland Publishers (UK) Ltd

All rights reserved. No part of this publication may be reproduced, stored in a retrieval system, or
transmitted in any form or by any means, electronic, mechanical, photocopying, recording or otherwise,
without the prior written permission of the publishers and copyright holders.

Gloucestershire County Library

992335485 7	
Askews	13-Feb-2003
717	£12.99

ISBN 1 84330 064 8 (hardback)

1 3 5 7 9 10 8 6 4 2

Editorial Direction: Rosemary Wilkinson
Project Editor: Clare Johnson
Production: Hazel Kirkman

Designed and created for New Holland by AG&G Books
Project design: AG&G Books   Project construction: AG&G Books and John Heming
Planting and props: AG&G Books and Vana Haggerty
Photography: AG&G Books and Ian Parsons   Illustrator: Gill Bridgewater
Editor: Fiona Corbridge   Designer: Glyn Bridgewater

Reproduction by Modern Age Repro House Ltd, Hong Kong
Printed and bound in Malaysia by Times Offset (M) Sdn. Bhd.

The information in this book is true and complete to the best of our knowledge. All recommendations are
made without guarantee on the part of the authors and the publishers. The authors and publishers
disclaim any liability for damages or injury resulting from the use of this information.

Conversion chart

To convert the metric measurements given in this book to imperial measurements, simply multiply the figure given in the text by the relevant number shown in the table alongside. Bear in mind that conversions will not necessarily work out exactly, and you will need to round the figure up or down slightly. (Do not use a combination of metric and imperial measurements – for accuracy, keep to one system.)

To convert	Multiply by
millimetres to inches	0.0394
metres to feet	3.28
metres to yards	1.093
sq millimetres to sq inches	0.00155
sq metres to sq feet	10.76
sq metres to sq yards	1.195
cu metres to cu feet	35.31
cu metres to cu yards	1.308
grams to pounds	0.0022
kilograms to pounds	2.2046
litres to gallons	0.22

Contents

Introduction

When we first entered the Cornish village that ringed the quayside cottage we eventually bought, we were amazed. Everything was built from local stone, from the houses, roofs, garden walls and gateposts to the harbour walls, steps, pavements, roads, paths and the slab in the butcher's shop. The scale of the more monumental structures, such as bridges and the giant battlements around the harbour, was naturally impressive; however, perhaps more than anything else, we were inspired by some of the more modest garden constructions – the low walls, the pretty arched seats, and the little flights of steps that tripped down to the water. From that moment on, we were captivated and inspired by the art and craft of stonework.

A dry-stone wall in a field in Ley, India, constructed using a mixture of giant boulders and small cobbles.

A brief history

If you could go back to the most primitive cave dwelling, you would find examples of stonework. Even though some structures were no more than heaps of stone – to contain a fire, or to form a worksurface – they still involved complex mind–eye–hand procedures of selecting and placing stones. And once people had learnt these skills, they graduated to creating walls, lintels, arches, houses and buildings on a much grander scale, such as pyramids and cathedrals.

Be inspired

Stonework is an exciting craft: once you have tried it, you will see the world with fresh eyes. Stone cottages, churches and country estates will fascinate you by showing what is possible when one stone is carefully placed upon another. Take the inspiration back home and translate it into items that will enrich and beautify your garden, giving you many hours of pleasure in the process.

Best of luck

An attractive rockery with a waterfall and pool. The large size of the rocks makes this a dramatic, natural-looking arrangement.

Health and safety

Many stoneworking procedures are potentially dangerous, so before starting work on the projects, check through the following list:

✔ Make sure that you are fit and strong enough for the task ahead of you. If you have doubts, ask your doctor for specific advice.

✔ When you are lifting large lumps of stone from ground level, minimize the risk of back strain by bending your knees, hugging the stone close to your body, and keeping the spine upright.

✔ If a slab of stone looks too heavy to lift on your own, ask others to help. Don't risk injury.

✔ Wear gloves, a dust-mask and goggles when you are handling cement and lime, or cutting stone with a hammer and chisel.

✔ Never operate a machine such as a power drill, or attempt a difficult lifting or manoeuvring task, if you are overtired or using medication.

✔ Keep a first-aid kit and telephone within easy reach.

Part 1

Techniques

Designing and planning

The secret of good stonework lies in the detail. If you are painstaking, and prepared to spend time thinking through the whole operation involved in a project – from measuring the site and making drawings, to ordering and buying stone, and considering how a seemingly immovable stone can be moved – then not only are you going to enjoy this book, but your garden will be magically transformed.

Looking at your outdoor space

Assessing your garden

Wander through your garden and observe how the position of the sun – the intensity of the light, and the depth of the shade – changes the mood of the space. Consider the possibilities. Could you blur the difference between indoor and outdoor space by constructing a stone patio right next to the house? Or change the way the garden is used by running a path in a new direction? Or encourage a different use of the space by building walls, tables and benches? There are many exciting alternatives.

Style considerations

Just as you style your interior decor – it might be modern, ethnic or period, for example – you need to do the same for your outdoor space. Do you simply want it to mirror the character of your indoor space? Or do you want it to be an adventurous reflection of nature?

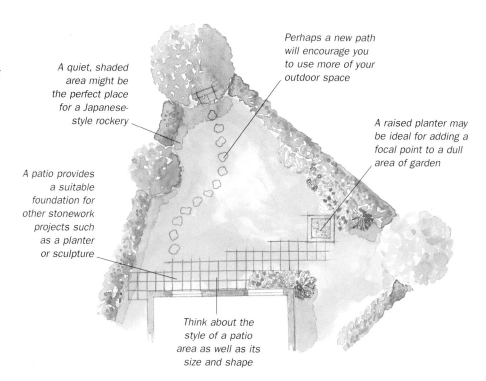

A quiet, shaded area might be the perfect place for a Japanese-style rockery

Perhaps a new path will encourage you to use more of your outdoor space

A raised planter may be ideal for adding a focal point to a dull area of garden

A patio provides a suitable foundation for other stonework projects such as a planter or sculpture

Think about the style of a patio area as well as its size and shape

Whatever the size, shape and style of your outdoor space, there are likely to be areas that you wish to improve. A patio may be essential, or you may want to build a dramatic stonework sculpture. Sketch out the possibilities on a plan of your garden.

Design

Deciding what to build

Once you have considered your outdoor space in terms of sunlight, mood and style, you can immerse yourself in the exciting business of deciding just what you want to build. The best way to proceed is to tackle the infrastructure first, and then take it from there. So if, for example, your garden lacks paths and paving, perhaps now is the time to do something about it. Then again, if you have always had an urge to build an arch or a wall, indulge in your dream.

Form and function

In many ways, it is true to say that form follows function – in the sense that you need to ensure that a bench is comfortable before you start to worry about the designer curlicues. However, don't let that stop you using your imagination. For example, if you like our Roman Arch Shrine (see page 88), but would prefer to build a whole row of shrines the full length of the garden, go ahead.

Choosing stone

Any stonework project has certain essential requirements – such as for thin slabs of stone or squarish blocks – but apart from that, various materials are usually suitable. To see what is on offer, visit suppliers who sell quarry stone, salvaged stone and reconstituted stone.

Drawing your designs

Once you have looked at your garden, and considered your needs in terms of design, size, function, stone supply and costs, turn to the projects. If you do not see exactly what you are looking for, sketch out your ideas and then work out how a project might be modified. Draw your design to a rough scale, complete with the number of courses of stone. A good way of planning out the building stages is to slice up the project into layers – the foundation slab, the first course of stone, the next course, and so on – and then draw the layers on paper. This will not only help clarify the order of work, but also reveal potential problems.

It is helpful to build up a picture scrapbook of stone structures, augmented by garden ephemera such as planters, that appeal to you. Use it for ideas and inspiration when planning a stonework design.

Planning

First steps

Plan out the logistics of the project. Firstly, decide where all the materials are going to be stored. If you are having stone delivered, ask if it will be offloaded on a pallet or whether you will be expected to help unload it by hand. Sometimes sand and gravel are delivered in huge bags, and unloaded with a hoist, so check that there is an adequate accessible space for them to live in. Where are you going to put the removed turf and waste earth?

Will the building procedures get in the way of all the other activities of the household, such as getting the car out, or children playing? Will you require help when it comes to mixing concrete or moving stone? Will you need to cover the

project with a plastic sheet if it starts to rain? Try to visualize every eventuality and forestall potential problems.

Permission and safety

Check that there are no planning restrictions governing the type of structure you are intending to build. If a project is constructed against a garden wall, check that the wall belongs to you. If it belongs to your neighbours, make sure that they have no objections before you go ahead.

For safety's sake, dress properly for the task ahead. You must protect your hands with strong gloves and your feet with heavy boots. Make sure that children are out of harm's way when you come to lifting heavy stones and slabs.

Planning checklist

✔ Is there a stone quarry in your area? This is likely to be the most economical source of materials.

✔ Is there adequate access to your garden? If the stone is unloaded in your driveway, or at your gate, will it cause problems or pose a danger?

✔ How are you going to move the stone to the site? Can you do it, or do you need friends to help?

✔ Is your garden reasonably level, with paths wide enough for a wheelbarrow? Or does it have soft, squashy lawns and very few pathways – if so, what arrangements do you need to make to move the materials?

Materials

For the projects in this book, all you really need to know about the primary materials – stone and sand – are their common names, colour and working characteristics. Once you know that sandstone splits into easy-to-work slices, and salvaged roof stone is good when you want to build a structure in thin courses, the rest is easy.

Caution

Stoneworkers risk injury from stones dropped on fingers or toes, and from muscle strain. Wear sturdy gloves and boots, lift carefully, and get help to move large stones.

Stone, concrete and mortar

Stone shape and colour

All the projects involve breaking stone with a chisel (rather than cutting with an angle grinder), so the two best types of stone to use are sandstone, which breaks into thin sheets, and limestone, which breaks into squarish blocks. Explain your needs to the supplier, see what stone is on offer, check its working characteristics, and then search around for pieces in the colour of your choice.

Natural stone versus reconstituted stone

The colour and texture of natural stone cannot be beaten; however, it is more expensive than reconstituted stone. For the most part, we prefer to use natural stone for walls and arrangements, and reconstituted stone when we need large, square-cut slabs or pavers. We did use reconstituted blocks for walling in the Dry-stone Border Wall (see page 46), but this is with the hope that once you have tried your hand with blocks, you will have the confidence to build a more complex wall project using natural stone.

Other materials

Soft sand (also known as builder's sand) is usually used for making smooth mortar, and sharp sand for making concrete and coarse-textured mortar. However, we use soft sand for most of the mortar mixes, and sharp sand in the form of ballast (a mixture of sand and gravel) when making concrete. This way of working enables you to buy the sand in bulk. Gravel and shingle are used both as decorative spreads and as a hardcore.

Buying stone

Decide on the colour and character of stone required for the project, and then visit a quarry or stoneyard and buy the stone as seen. Most stone is sold by the square metre or cubic metre. Pick out the pieces and spread them on the ground to fill up a square metre – this allows you to see how the pieces relate to each other for the purposes of the project. Never buy stone without looking at it first.

Opposite page: A selection of materials suitable for making the projects in this book (reconstituted stone products are available at builders' merchants):
1 Reconstituted stone block, 2 Concrete block, 3 Reconstituted stone rope-top edging, 4 Corner post 5 Celtic pattern paver and square paver, 6 Ceramic roof tile, 7 Limestone, 8 Sandstone, 9 Brick, 10 Roof stone, 11 Flagstone, 12 Medium-sized cobble, 13 Reconstituted stone paver, 14 York stone, 15 Statue, 16 Rock, 17 Slate chippings, 18 Radius paving, 19 Pea gravel, 20 Feature stone, 21 Reconstituted stone paver, 22 Reconstituted grey stone setts.

Concrete and mortar mixes

Mortar and concrete both contain aggregates, cement and water, but are made according to quite different recipes. Most stoneworkers have their own favourite blends. For example, some people make mortar using 1 part cement, 5 parts coarse sharp sand and 1 part lime; others use 1 part cement, 6 parts soft sand, and don't bother with the lime. The quantities we give in the projects are generous and allow for wastage. We use the following mixes:

Caution
Cement and lime are both corrosive
Always wear a dust-mask, gloves and goggles. If you get cement or lime powder on your skin – especially if your skin is damp – wash it off immediately with copious amounts of water.

- Concrete for general foundations: 1 part Portland cement to 5 parts ballast (ranging from small stones down to sharp sand).
- Concrete for paths: 1 part Portland cement to 4 parts ballast.
- Mortar for a general mix: 1 part Portland cement to 4 parts soft sand.
- Mortar for a smooth, strong mix: 1 part Portland cement, 1 part lime, and 3–4 parts soft sand.

Tools

Tools are one of the main keys to successful stonework. Although the best tools are no substitute for enthusiasm and determination, carefully chosen, top-quality tools will ensure that each and every task is accomplished with minimum effort and maximum efficiency, in the shortest possible time. However, it is fine to begin by using existing tools for the projects – just buy new ones if and when the need arises.

Choosing and using the correct tools

Measuring and marking

You need a flexible tape measure and a straight-edge for measuring the site, a rule for taking smaller measurements within the project, pegs and string for setting out the shape of the project on the ground, a spirit level to check that the project is both vertically and horizontally level, and a piece of chalk for drawing registration marks. It will make your life easier if you have two tape measures – a small, steel one for making measurements up to 3 m, and a large, wipe-clean fibreglass tape for measuring over longer distances in the garden.

Moving earth

Get yourself a spade for slicing into grass and for digging holes, and a fork for picking up turf. To move earth from one spot to another, you need a shovel, a wheelbarrow, and one or more buckets. If you are moving a lot of earth, it is a good idea to obtain a rake for spreading out the earth on the site.

Cutting and breaking stone

Apart from strong gloves to safeguard your hands and stout boots to protect your feet, you will require a sledgehammer for compacting hardcore level, a club hammer and bolster chisel for cutting and splitting stone, and a mason's hammer for the more precise task of cutting and pecking small pieces of stone to shape. An old piece of carpet makes a good surface to work on. For cleaning the stone and tidying up the site at the end of work, it is handy to have a wire brush, broom and a small hand brush. If you are prone to suffer from aches and pains, especially in your knees, it is a good idea to use an old cushion or padded kneeling mat to kneel on while you work.

Mixing concrete and mortar

You need a shovel for moving the sand, cement and ballast, a bucket for carrying water and small amounts of the concrete or mortar mixture, and a wheelbarrow for moving large amounts of the mixture around the garden. If you discover that you really enjoy working with stone and intend to do a lot of it, a small electric mixer will make the task of mixing concrete and mortar a lot easier. Always wash mortar and concrete off tools as soon as you have finished working, especially in hot weather when the mixtures are liable to harden quickly.

Laying stone

Once the concrete and mortar have been moved to the site, you must have a bricklayer's trowel (a large trowel) for handling large amounts of mortar, and a pointing trowel (a small trowel) for tidying up the joints and making good. We also use the bricklayer's trowel to carry the mortar when we are using the pointing trowel to do the pointing. When the stone is nicely bedded on the mortar, it is tapped into place with a club hammer or a rubber mallet. The measurements and levels are checked to make sure that they are correct. Finally, about an hour after the stone has been laid, when the mortar has started to cure, the excess mortar is removed with a trowel.

General tasks

At various points along the way, we use a claw hammer for banging in and pulling out nails, a crosscut saw for sizing lengths of wood, a portable drill in conjunction with drill bits for drilling holes and a screwdriver bit for driving in screws, and a craft knife to cut string and plastic sheet. We use all manner of odd-shaped pieces of plywood and board for protecting the site and as workboards to hold piles of mortar. If you value your existing lawn, start the project by surrounding the site with workboards so that the grass is covered and safeguarded from damage by feet, wheelbarrows and tools.

Caution
Power tools

Electricity, early-morning dew, buckets of water and wet hands are a potentially dangerous combination. If you do decide to use a power drill instead of a portable drill, or an electric cement mixer, make sure that you use them in conjunction with an electricity circuit breaker, which will protect you against possible electric shock.

A basic tool kit

For making the projects in this book, you will need the tools shown below. All of these can be bought from a local general DIY superstore, or hired from a hire shop. The angle grinder is optional – it is quite expensive and not essential for the projects. However, if you are planning to do a lot of stonework projects in the future which involve cutting stone, it may be a worthwhile investment. Likewise, an electric cement mixer (not illustrated) may also be useful.

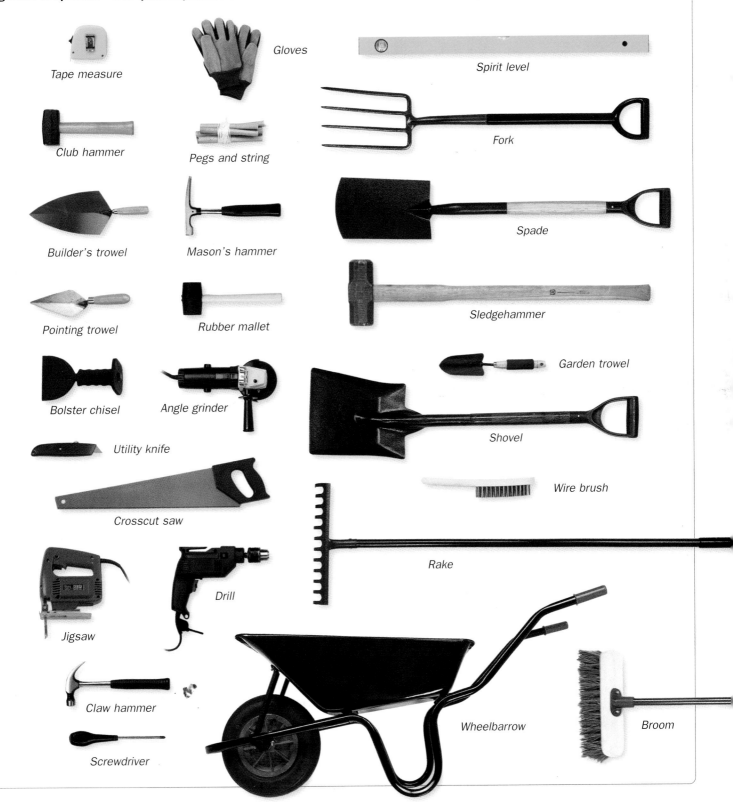

Tape measure

Gloves

Spirit level

Club hammer

Pegs and string

Fork

Builder's trowel

Mason's hammer

Spade

Pointing trowel

Rubber mallet

Sledgehammer

Bolster chisel

Angle grinder

Garden trowel

Utility knife

Shovel

Crosscut saw

Wire brush

Jigsaw

Drill

Rake

Claw hammer

Screwdriver

Wheelbarrow

Broom

Basic techniques

Once you have mastered the basic techniques, working with stone is a wonderfully therapeutic experience. After a day or so of practising the basic techniques, such as cutting stone and mixing mortar, you will be able to tackle any of the projects in this book. And after a weekend of putting your skills into practice, you will see a fascinating structure emerge from a heap of stone and a pile of sand.

Marking out

When you have chosen your site and made sure that it is right for the project, measure out the area needed and mark it with pegs and string. If the foundation is square or rectilinear, check that corners are at right angles by making sure that the two diagonal measurements are identical. The two-peg technique at the corners (see photo on the right) not only allows you to set out the shape without cutting the string, but also to dig the trench without the pegs getting in the way. Use a natural-fibre string that is less likely to twist and knot itself.

Make sure the strings cross at right angles

You can choose to wet the string prior to use so that it shrinks and tightens on the pegs

Use pegs and string to mark out the size and shape of a site. Double-check your measurements every step of the way.

Preparing a foundation

Rock the ends of the batten against the top edge of the formwork

You may need to add or remove concrete to achieve the correct level

Use a frame of wood (formwork) set level in the ground to establish the area for the concrete slab. Fill the formwork with concrete and tamp and scrape it level.

Building formwork

With the shape of the foundation marked with pegs and string, dig out the earth to the required depth and move it from the site. Take the formwork boards and formwork pegs, and set to work building a frame within the recess. Bang two pegs in the ground, set one board level against the pegs and screw it in place. Position the second board against the first and fix it with pegs, then continue until the frame is complete.

Use the spirit level to check that the top edge of the frame is level. If it is necessary to hit the frame slightly to adjust the level, be sure to remove the spirit level first so that it doesn't get hit with the hammer by accident.

Laying the concrete slab

When the formwork has been built, spread your chosen hardcore – it might be broken stone or builder's rubble – within the frame and use the sledgehammer to stamp it into the ground. Avoid using rubble that contains vegetable matter, bits and pieces of rusty iron or glass. Never use anything that contains asbestos. Continue until you have a firm, compact layer of hardcore.

Starting from one end of the formwork, pour concrete over the hardcore. Spread it roughly with the shovel, and use a length of wood to tamp it level with the top of the formwork. The general rule with concrete is the dryer the mix, the stronger the finished concrete slab.

Use a bolster chisel and a club hammer to cut (break) pieces of stone. Hold the chisel upright and hit it several times.

Cutting stone

Using a bolster chisel

A bolster chisel and club hammer are used to break stones in two. Mark the line of cut with a straight-edge and a piece of chalk. Wear gloves to guard your hands and goggles to protect your eyes. Keep children and pets out of the way because of the danger of flying shards of stone. Place the stone on a block of wood, a pad of old carpet or even a pile of sand, set the bolster chisel on the line, and give it a series of taps with the club hammer. Repeat this procedure on both sides of the stone to score a line. Now increase the force of the blow until the stone breaks in two. Don't be tempted to try and break the stone with a single, crashing blow – it rarely works!

Using a mason's hammer

A mason's hammer is used to trim stones to shape. Hold the stone firmly in one hand, so that the edge to be trimmed is furthest away from you. Take the mason's hammer and use the chisel end of the head to clip the edge into shape.

Building

Laying courses of stone

Mix the mortar to a smooth, buttery consistency, so that it is firm without being watery. Dampen the pile of stone. Trowel mortar on the foundation slab and set the first stone in place. Butter the end of the next stone with mortar and bed it into the mortar on the slab, with its end butted hard up against the first stone. When you have a line of stones, take a club hammer or rubber mallet and gently tap the stones into line. Don't fuss around with the mortar that oozes out, other than to gather it up and throw it back on the pile. Make sure that bits of hard mortar and stone do not get thrown back into the mortar heap.

Levelling the courses

When you have put down a group of stones, it is necessary to check and adjust the vertical and horizontal levels. Stand back and try to identify problems, then put a wooden batten on the stones, and tap it with the hammer until the offending stones get into line. Place the spirit level against the batten to take a reading, then make further adjustments if needed.

When you are laying courses of stone, remember to stagger the joints and check each course is level before proceeding.

Filling joints

After filling crazy-paving joints with mortar, use a pointing trowel to shape the mortar into an angled or slightly peaked finish.

Filling joints

When you have finished a section of wall, the cavities need to be filled or pointed. Use the small pointing trowel to spread a 10 mm layer of buttery mortar over the back of the large bricklayer's trowel. Using the large trowel as your palette and the small trowel like a spatula, slice through the mortar to reveal a straight edge, and then pick up a 10 mm-wide strip on the back edge of the small trowel (so that you have a square-section worm) and wipe it into the cavity. Follow the procedure on all open joints. This is a skill that needs to be practised. Hold the trowels in the way that is most comfortable for you, and you will be more likely to get good results.

Pointing and raking joints

You can either wait until the mortar is firm and then use the trowel to tool it to a smooth, shaped finish, or you can wait until the mortar is hard and rake out the joints to reveal the edges of the stone. Most projects in this book favour the raking option. Do not be tempted to rake out mortar while it is still soft.

Paths, steps and patios

Paths, steps and patios are functionally desirable in that they provide dry, level areas enabling us to move around the garden in comfort. They are also visually desirable – who can resist exploring a path that curves out of sight, or climbing steps that lead up a slope, or sitting on a shaded patio? Visit parks, gardens and stately homes to get an idea of possibilities for schemes varying from the simple to the grandiose.

Constructing paths

Designing and planning

Study the site and decide on the route and the type of path, including the depth and structure of the foundation, and the type of surface material and edging required. Use the tape measure, pegs and string to mark out the route on the ground. Make sure that the layout does not upset the balance of the garden.

Building

Dig out the earth to the required depth, spread compacted hardcore over the site and top it with your chosen surface – sand, ballast or concrete. If the ground is soft and/or wet, a firmer foundation is needed, so dig out the earth to a greater depth, increase the thickness of the hardcore, and use concrete rather than sand or ballast. Bed the stone, pavers or slabs on generous blobs of mortar. Dig a trench and bed the edging in mortar. Finally, fill the joints with sand or mortar.

This beautifully crafted, natural-looking path is built from Gloucestershire stone. The stones are set on edge (a traditional technique) in a mixture of clay and crushed stone. The path may be a little bumpy to walk on, but would look good in a traditional garden. Curved or undulating paths can also be built using the same technique.

INSPIRATIONS

A mixture of brick pavers and stone lends itself to rectangular layouts.

The precise shapes of moulded concrete slabs allow you to create complex patterns.

Natural stone steps edged by rockery stones are ideal for a fairly informal garden.

Constructing steps

Designing and planning

Decide on the number and height of the risers, and the depth of the treads. Measure the average thickness of the stone you intend to use and see how many courses you need for each riser.

Building

Use pegs and string to set out the foundation, then dig to the required depth, set the formwork in the recess and fill it with hardcore and concrete. Build the first riser and side walls and back-fill with hardcore. Set the first tread in place. Build subsequent steps in the same way.

These rockery steps are like stepping stones and seem to be part of the landscape. The design of more formal steps needs careful planning with a tape measure, batten and spirit level.

Constructing a patio

This blue-grey patio is made of random pieces of slate laid as crazy paving. It includes a circular feature made of stones set on edge in a radiating pattern, looking like a fossilized ammonite.

Designing and planning

Use the tape measure, string and pegs to describe the shape of the patio on the ground. If you are using cast concrete pavers, do your best to make sure that the patio is made up from a number of whole units, so that you don't have to cut slabs.

Building

Dig the foundation to the required depth and set the formwork in place. Check the levels and adjust the formwork so that there is a very slight fall to one side, so the patio will shed surface water. Spread the hardcore and sand, ballast or concrete. Bed the surface material on mortar.

Recessed steps, together with symmetrical decorative urns, give a classical feel to an area.

A patio area and path made from stone pavers, stepping stones, cobbles and gravel.

A circular patio and a radiating design attract attention and so become a focal point.

Walls and other structures

Walls, containers, pedestals and other freestanding structures are usually built from courses of stone and extra care is needed to build strong, safe structures that will not fall down. Once completed, there is a good chance that they will still be in existence in a hundred years' time. Walls are capable of making a powerful statement in your garden, with aesthetic possibilities as well as practical advantages.

Constructing walls

Designing and planning

Decide where you want the wall. Do you want a dry-stone wall or are you going to use mortar? Do you want an easy-to-build low wall (such as a three-course wall across the corner of the garden), or a more complex freestanding structure that needs a substantial foundation?

Once you have decided on the height, form and construction, sit down with a pencil and paper and work out the quantities of stone, sand and cement.

Building

Use a tape measure, pegs and string to establish the shape of the foundation trench. Dig the trench, half-fill it with hardcore and top it with concrete. Select stone for the first two or three courses and have a dry run to test placement. Then either lay the stones with mud pug if it is a dry-stone wall (see the Dry-stone Border Wall on page 46), or use mortar.

This dry-stone wall in Wales is made from chunky slabs of slate. Note how the builder has selected and placed the stones to create a strong and attractive pattern.

INSPIRATIONS

Mixed materials and built-in shelves provide a beautiful backdrop for pot plants.

This stone wall with decorative coping (top pieces) could make a good garden boundary wall.

A seating area achieved by incorporating large, outward-extending slabs into the wall.

Constructing containers

A container made from a single piece of found stone. Not everyone is lucky enough to find a piece of naturally hollowed stone such as this, but it is possible to make your own using hypertufa (see the Japanese Suiseki Stone on page 34).

Designing and planning

Establish the shape, height and composition of the container. Decide whether it needs a foundation, such as a slab, a trench full of hardcore, or a trench with hardcore and concrete, and then use the tape measure, pegs and string to mark the shape of the foundation on the ground.

Building

Once the foundation is in place, take your chosen stone and set out the first two or three courses dry, choosing the best possible stones for the corners. Fix the courses in place with mortar.

Constructing columns and pedestals

Designing, planning and building

Columns and pedestals are really just small containers with the centres filled in, so you can follow the same designing, planning and building procedures already described. Build with extra care and attention, especially when it comes to checking the horizontal and vertical levels, because tiny inaccuracies are swiftly accentuated and highlighted by the modest size of the structure. Remember that there is always a correlation between the height of the structure and the size of the foundation. If you want to build a tall structure (more than 1 m high) the foundation needs to be proportionally wider.

As an alternative to building a pedestal from lots of small pieces of stone, you can search around for large, ready-made pieces. Here, saddle stones (used for the base of a haystack) form striking pedestals for displaying plant pots or ornaments.

Decorative stone containers, full of plants, add interest and warmth to a plain paved area.

A bold stone structure is sometimes all that is needed to decorate your yard.

A two-tier pedestal for displaying plants, which could also form a retaining wall.

Rockeries and other stone arrangements

Rockeries are built in direct imitation of nature; other garden stone arrangements are often built as a contrast or may even have a symbolic purpose, containing spheres, cones or Japanese lanterns, for example. Look at stones in nature, art and architecture, and then draw inspiration from your observations.

Constructing a rockery

A striking rockery and waterfall. The large rocks have been positioned in imitation of a natural rocky slope. (If you want to make a rockery avoiding the use of huge rocks, see the Traditional Rockery project on page 26, which uses thin layers of stone instead.)

Designing and planning

To give you ideas for constructing a natural-looking rockery, think about the beaches and mountains you have visited. Use a tape measure, pegs and string to map the shape of the rockery on the ground. Remember that if you are going to use huge rocks, you have to find some way of getting them to the site. It may be easier to group small rocks, which are relatively easy to move, so that they look like large outcrops.

Building

Clear the site of all weeds and cover it with shale, hardcore or shingle. Arrange the rocks in groups or stacks, and tilt them so that they rear up at an angle. Create small pockets of rich soil all over the site, for filling with rockery plants. Cover a good proportion of the rocks and soil with your chosen grit, pea gravel or crushed shell.

INSPIRATIONS

A miniature version of a stony landscape will blend well into almost any small garden.

This arrangement of bold plants bordered by large rocks looks like a natural outcrop.

A design using ground-covering stone, plants and rocks to mimic a river and its banks.

A beautifully built cone, which may not be particularly useful, but is a great piece of sculpture for the garden! Any bold shape like this will probably dominate a small garden, so make sure you really want one.

An award-winning Japanese-style garden (Gold medal winner at the Hampton Court Flower Festival, England, 1995). A "river" of stone flows beneath a simple stone bridge and around other small feature stones – a landscape in miniature.

Japanese-style arrangements

Designing and building

For the Japanese, the art of rock arrangement is concerned with using a small number of stones to create a blend of nature and symbolism, and each and every stone that plays a part needs to be chosen with great care. When creating your own version try, if possible, to use timeworn stones covered in moss and lichen, which impart subtle colour, shape and character to the arrangement.

Sculptures and other found objects

Designing and building

The wonderful thing about using stone sculptures and found stones is that you can follow your intuition and create an arrangement that is uniquely your own. If you like stone frogs or gnomes, or have a passion for collecting pebbles, you are halfway to having a very special rock garden. Set aside a corner – perhaps an area ringed with rocks – and then simply set out your sculptures and found stones, allowing the arrangement to evolve.

A traditional Japanese design that uses bamboo to deliver water to a stone basin.

A simple path design is remarkably powerful when placed in stark surroundings.

A "river" of randomly shaped stones forms an attractive path and is also easy to build.

Part 2
Projects

Traditional rockery

Anyone who is lucky enough to have a natural outcrop of rock in the garden has the perfect place for planting beautiful heathers, alpines and lichens. You can create the same effect by building a rockery with lots of nooks and crannies for rock plants. The great thing about this project is the fact that the rockery is made from small, easy-to-handle stones, which can be transported in your car without difficulty.

Easy

Making time
One weekend
*One day for clearing
the site and setting
the rocks in place, and
one day for planting*

Considering the design

It would be nice if you could wave a magic wand and conjure up a series of dramatic monolithic rocks in your garden. However, the expense, physical challenge and access difficulties involved in moving large single rocks into an established garden make most people shy away from the prospect. It's much easier to build a rockery from small, manageable rocks, and we have designed the project with this in mind.

The slices of rock are stacked like slices of bread, and arranged to resemble the tip of a sloping outcrop of stone breaking through the ground. Note how the groups of stones are placed in steps, and the line of steps both rears up and angles across the bed. The borders of the rockery are defined by stones set on edge.

Getting started

Walk around your garden and look at the various possible sites. Ideally, you need a site that is gently sloping, well drained, and has no overhanging trees. It should receive plenty of sun, because many rockery plants prefer these conditions.

You will need

Tools

- Tape measure
- Pegs and string
- Spade, fork, rake and shovel
- Wheelbarrow and bucket
- Club hammer

Materials

For a rockery 2 m long and 1 m wide

- York stone: about 3 sq. m of split sandstone, in the largest sizes that you can manage (rockery stones)
- York stone: about 2 sq. m of split sandstone in random small sizes (coping edging)
- Shingle: 300 kg of large-size, well-washed shingle
- Pea gravel: 100 kg of well-washed gravel in a colour to match the stone
- Planting mixture: 1 part (50 kg) topsoil, 1 part (50 kg) fine grit, gravel or stone chippings, 1 part (50 kg) leaf mould
- Rockery plants (such as erica, sedum, alyssum, aubretia, campanula, cerastium, erigeron, primula, saponaria, sempervivum, saxifrage, thyme; bulbs such as dwarf narcissus, crocus, cyclamen, chionodoxa, muscari, galanthus and convallaria)

Overall dimensions and general notes

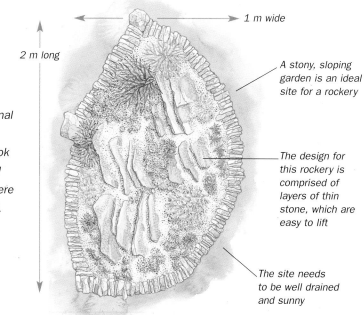

1 m wide

2 m long

A small, traditional rockery of this character will look good in a typical town garden where space is limited.

A stony, sloping garden is an ideal site for a rockery

The design for this rockery is comprised of layers of thin stone, which are easy to lift

The site needs to be well drained and sunny

Cut-away view of the traditional rockery

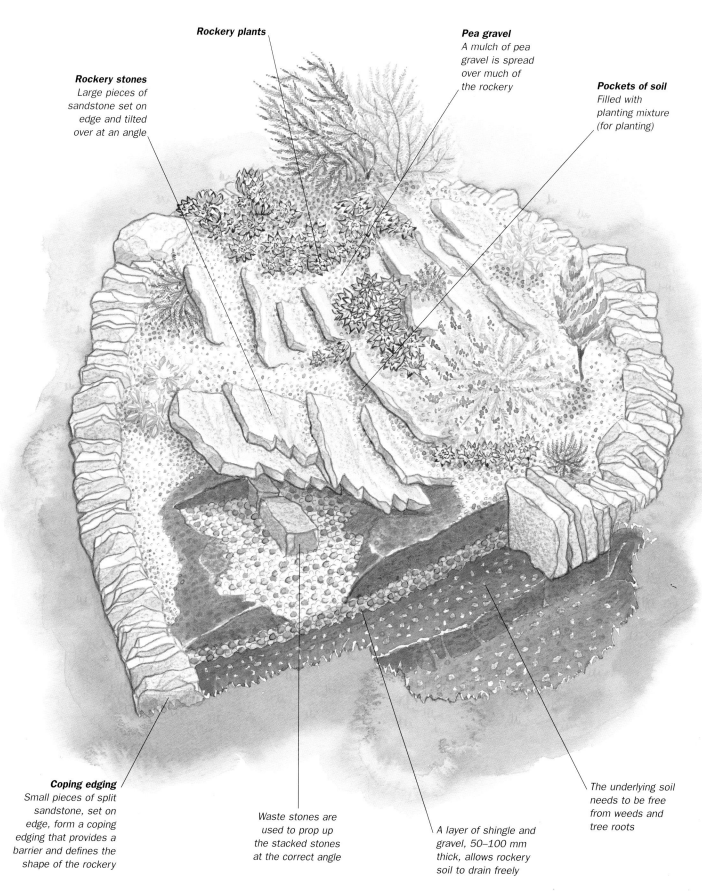

Rockery plants

Pea gravel
A mulch of pea gravel is spread over much of the rockery

Rockery stones
Large pieces of sandstone set on edge and tilted over at an angle

Pockets of soil
Filled with planting mixture (for planting)

Coping edging
Small pieces of split sandstone, set on edge, form a coping edging that provides a barrier and defines the shape of the rockery

Waste stones are used to prop up the stacked stones at the correct angle

A layer of shingle and gravel, 50–100 mm thick, allows rockery soil to drain freely

The underlying soil needs to be free from weeds and tree roots

Making the traditional rockery

1 Measuring out
Measure out the area for the rockery, clear the turf and weeds, and define it with a simple coping made from stones set on edge. Dig over the site and increase the drainage by adding a small amount of shingle and pea gravel to the earth.

2 Covering with shingle
Rake shingle and pea gravel over the whole site to a depth of about 50–100 mm. Tread it into the soil, until the entire area feels firm underfoot.

3 Stacking the stone
Stack the split sandstone rockery stones side by side, in groups of three or four slices. Arrange the leading edges of the stones so that the profiles look natural in relation to each other.

4 Stabilizing the rockery
Use pieces of waste stone to prop up the stacks of stone so that they all rear up at the same angle. Pack additional shingle under the stacks to make them stable and firm.

5 Adding soil
Rake the planting mixture over the whole arrangement and pack it under the stones. Look for natural planting areas, and make sure that they are covered by a generous thickness of soil.

6 Planting
Purchase suitable rockery plants. Spend time considering the best possible arrangement before you plant them. Water them in, and water regularly until established.

Magic knot path

If you enjoy colour and Celtic imagery, this path will appeal. It is a good, strong, formal path, which is hardwearing and long-lasting. The imitation York stone flags and terracotta trim (both made from concrete) ensure a firm, non-slippery surface. The path is made up from three component parts: a basic flagstone, a Celtic knot strip, and a Celtic corner square (used in a central position in the design).

★
Easy

Making time
Two weekends
Two days for laying the concrete, and two days for laying the slabs and making good

Considering the design

The pattern consists of a number of repeats, each comprising two flagstones surrounded by three strips and a single corner square. The path is 1.074 m wide. The length of the strips allows the slabs to be set in place with an all-round joint width of about 6 mm.

Getting started

Decide how long you want your path to be. Divide the total length by 612 mm to work out how many repeats you need, and then multiply the number of components in the repeat to give you the total amounts of materials required.

Overall dimensions and general notes

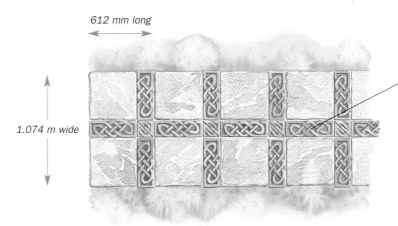

612 mm long

1.074 m wide

The design can be changed to suit your needs (the paving strips could run either side of the path instead of down the middle)

This bold, colourful path works well in many styles of garden, from minimalist modern spaces to traditional cottage plots. The design is only suitable for a straight path.

You will need

Tools

- ✔ Tape measure and straight-edge
- ✔ Pegs and string
- ✔ Spade, fork and shovel
- ✔ Wheelbarrow and bucket
- ✔ Crosscut saw
- ✔ Claw hammer
- ✔ Club hammer
- ✔ Sledgehammer
- ✔ Tamping beam: about 1.5 m long, 60 mm wide and 30 mm thick
- ✔ Bricklayer's trowel
- ✔ Spirit level

- ✔ Rubber mallet
- ✔ Pointing trowel
- ✔ Soft-bristled brush

Materials

All quantities are per 612 mm of path (1 repeat). Path is 1.074 m wide

- ✔ Reconstituted York stone paving slabs: 2 slabs, 450 mm square
- ✔ Celtic knot terracotta paving strips: 3 strips, 462 mm long, 150 mm wide and 38 mm thick
- ✔ Celtic knot terracotta corner square: 1 piece, 150 mm square and 38 mm thick

- ✔ Pine boards: length to suit your path, 150 mm wide and 20 mm thick (formwork)
- ✔ Pine battens: length to suit width of your path, 30 mm wide and 20 mm thick (expansion battens, tamping beam and formwork pegs)
- ✔ Hardcore: 2 wheelbarrow loads
- ✔ Concrete: 1 part (14 kg) cement, 3 parts (42 kg) ballast
- ✔ Mortar: 1 part (10 kg) cement, 2 parts (20 kg) soft sand
- ✔ Nails: 1 kg of 38 mm-long nails

Cut-away view of the magic knot path

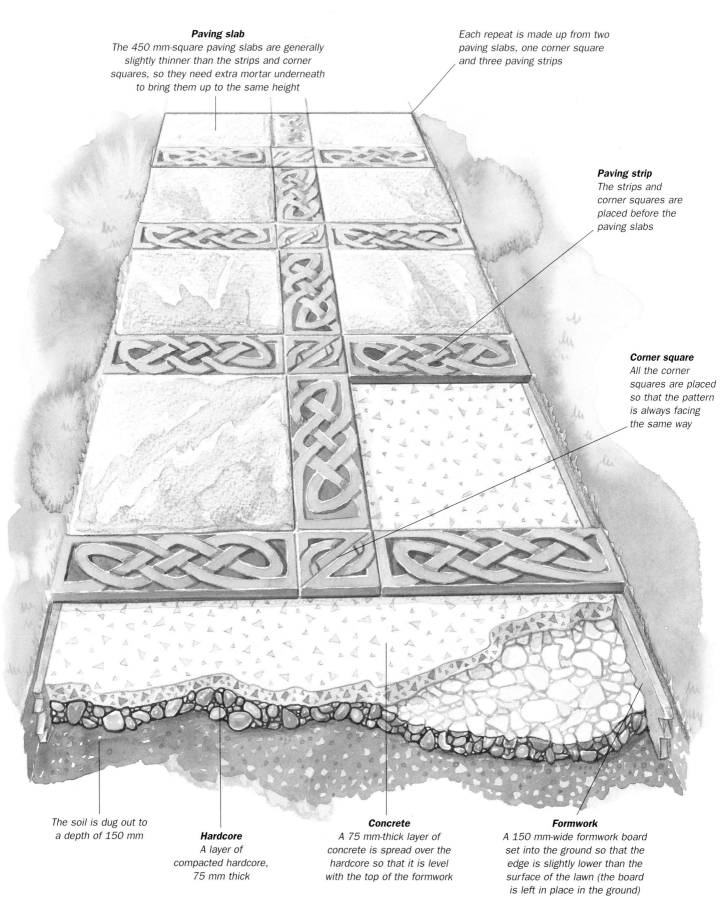

Paving slab
The 450 mm-square paving slabs are generally slightly thinner than the strips and corner squares, so they need extra mortar underneath to bring them up to the same height

Each repeat is made up from two paving slabs, one corner square and three paving strips

Paving strip
The strips and corner squares are placed before the paving slabs

Corner square
All the corner squares are placed so that the pattern is always facing the same way

The soil is dug out to a depth of 150 mm

Hardcore
A layer of compacted hardcore, 75 mm thick

Concrete
A 75 mm-thick layer of concrete is spread over the hardcore so that it is level with the top of the formwork

Formwork
A 150 mm-wide formwork board set into the ground so that the edge is slightly lower than the surface of the lawn (the board is left in place in the ground)

Making the magic knot path

1 Setting up the formwork
Mark out the path, making it 1.074 m wide. Dig out the earth to a depth of 150 mm. Put the formwork boards in the recess, nailing them with the claw hammer and fixing them in place with the formwork pegs. Compact a 75 mm layer of hardcore on the path.

2 Filling with concrete
Set expansion battens every 2–3 metres across the width of the path to allow for expansion of the concrete. Mix the concrete to a thick consistency. Shovel it over the hardcore and use the tamping beam to tamp it level with the top edge of the formwork.

3 Establishing guidelines
Use string to mark out a guideline at one side of the path. Placing the paving strips against this, set out another guideline 462 mm in from the side to mark the position of the corner squares in the centre of the path.

4 Laying the strips
Mix the mortar to a stiff, buttery consistency and lay the corner squares and paving strips down the centre of the path. Use the spirit level and rubber mallet to ensure that they are level.

5 Laying the paving slabs
Lay each York stone paving slab by setting five generous, bun-sized blobs of mortar on the path. Position the slabs so that they are level with the paving strips. Make sure that the joints are consistently 6 mm wide.

6 Pointing
Finally, mix a small amount of mortar to a dry, crumbly consistency, and brush and trowel it into the joints. Wait about four hours and then brush all surplus mortar off the path.

Japanese suiseki stone

Traditional Japanese gardens make great use of stone for ornamental and symbolic purposes. One such stone is termed a *suiseki* – meaning a large, natural basin. Our suiseki combines Japanese heritage with the very English craft of making stone-like containers from hypertufa, which is a mixture of moss, sand and cement. If you like the notion of East meeting West, this project will add oriental tranquillity to your garden.

★
Easy

Making time
One weekend
One day for casting the stone, and one day for arranging the stone and the cobbles

Overall dimensions and general notes

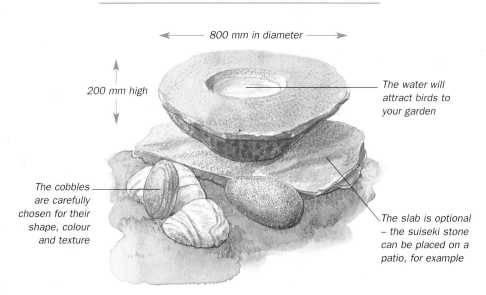

←——— 800 mm in diameter ———→

200 mm high

The water will attract birds to your garden

The cobbles are carefully chosen for their shape, colour and texture

The slab is optional – the suiseki stone can be placed on a patio, for example

The suiseki will look good in slightly wild settings; also in a modern garden or courtyard. It is a traditional element in Japanese gardens, which are famed for their relaxing qualities.

You will need

Tools
- ✔ Workboard: 1 m square
- ✔ Wheelbarrow
- ✔ Shovel
- ✔ Bucket
- ✔ Bricklayer's trowel
- ✔ Tape measure and a spirit level
- ✔ Wire snips
- ✔ Paintbrush

Materials
For a suiseki stone 800 mm in diameter and 200 mm high

- ✔ Hypertufa mix:
  1 part (25 kg) cement,
  1 part (25 kg) sharp sand,
  2 parts (50 kg) sphagnum moss
- ✔ Bowl: metal or plastic, 300 mm in diameter at the rim, 170 mm in diameter at the base, and 100 mm in height
- ✔ Bar of kitchen soap
- ✔ Wire grid mesh: 25 mm mesh, about 400 mm square
- ✔ Mortar: 1 part (2 kg) cement, 3 parts (6 kg) soft sand
- ✔ Resin: about 4 cupfuls of waterproofing medium
- ✔ Cobbles for decoration

Considering the design

This is one of the easiest projects in the book – the suiseki stone emerges after a straightforward process which really only involves pressing the hypertufa mix over an upturned bowl to create a cast basin. However, the simplicity of its creation belies the finished effect – once the basin is displayed with one or two specimen rocks and stones, and shown off against a subtle backdrop of carefully chosen plants, perhaps in a quiet and protected corner of the garden, it comes into its own as an object of surprising beauty. In a Japanese garden, the suiseki symbolizes the refreshing and purifying aspects of nature, such as dew on a leaf, or water in the cleft of a rock.

The suiseki is about 800 mm wide at the rim and 200 mm tall, and the under-cut and textured underside contrasts with the smooth and level top surface.

Getting started

Start searching for a smooth plastic or metal bowl that is wider at the rim than at the base. We used a stainless-steel bowl found in a charity shop, 300 mm in diameter at the rim, 170 mm in diameter at the base, and 100 mm in height.

Cross-section of the Japanese suiseki stone during construction (the stone is upside-down)

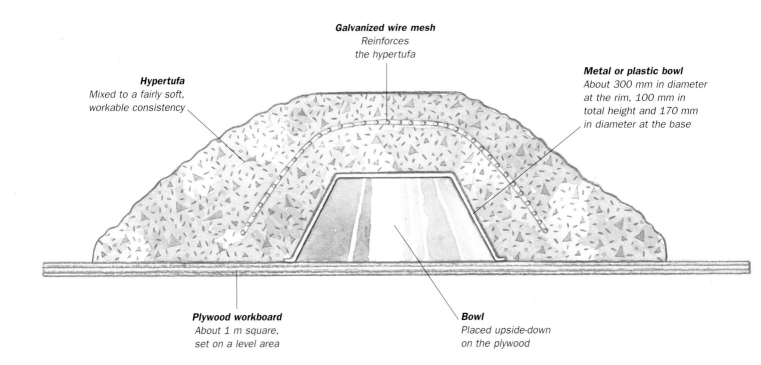

Galvanized wire mesh
Reinforces the hypertufa

Hypertufa
Mixed to a fairly soft, workable consistency

Metal or plastic bowl
About 300 mm in diameter at the rim, 100 mm in total height and 170 mm in diameter at the base

Plywood workboard
About 1 m square, set on a level area

Bowl
Placed upside-down on the plywood

Cut-away view of the Japanese suiseki stone

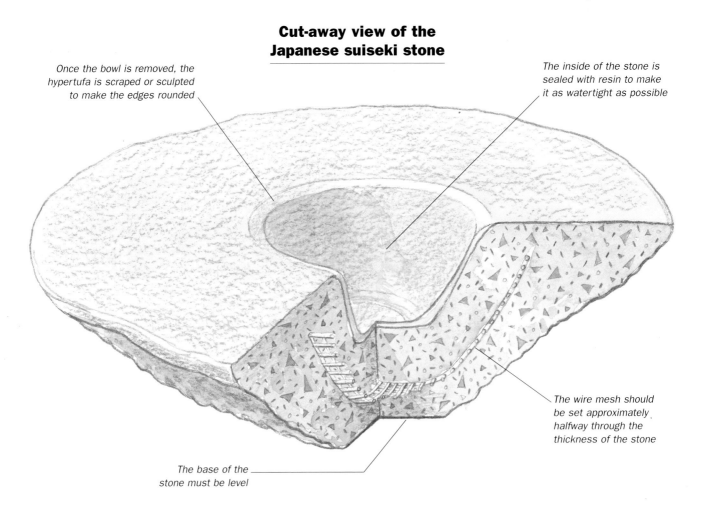

Once the bowl is removed, the hypertufa is scraped or sculpted to make the edges rounded

The inside of the stone is sealed with resin to make it as watertight as possible

The wire mesh should be set approximately halfway through the thickness of the stone

The base of the stone must be level

Making the Japanese suiseki stone

1 **Mixing the hypertufa**
Wipe the outside of the bowl with a small amount of water and a lot of soap, until it is slippery. Set it upside-down on the workboard. Mix the hypertufa ingredients with water to form a soft consistency, and start spreading a layer of it over the bowl.

2 **Inserting the wire mesh**
Build up a layer of hypertufa about 70 mm thick, then cut the wire mesh to fit over the mound and press it in. All the edges should be embedded and it must be a tight, close-hugging fit.

3 **Completing the mound**
Continue adding hypertufa until the wire mesh is completely covered. Aim for a mound that is irregular in shape and about 800 mm in diameter at the widest part of the rim. Run the trowel round the rim to smooth it.

4 **Texturing the surface**
Level the top of the mound so that the finished basin will sit flat when it is flipped over. Use your fingers to knead and texture the surface of the sides so that it looks weathered and worn.

5 **Painting with resin**
When the hypertufa is dry, turn the mound over and remove the bowl. Wipe the inside of the depression with mortar. When it has dried, paint a coat of resin over the mortar to make it waterproof.

6 **Setting up the suiseki**
Continue to make the surface of the hypertufa look like weathered stone by scratching and scraping it. Finally, set the suiseki level on your chosen slab of stone, fill it with water, and decorate it with cobbles and plants.

Old English random paving

If you are intending to build a patio, but do not want to use identical square paving slabs or tessellating blocks, Old English random paving is a good option. It is easy to lay, functional, and the subtle repeat pattern looks good. Although the style is "Old English", the slabs are very modern reconstituted stone. This patio is 3 m square, which gives plenty of space for a table and chairs, or a couple of sun loungers.

★
Easy

Making time
One weekend
One day for setting out the formwork; one day for laying the concrete and the slabs

Considering the design

The design is based on a 300 mm grid. The patio is made from three sizes of reconstituted York stone slab: twelve large squares, eighteen half-squares, and sixteen quarter-squares. However if you wish, the emphasis of the pattern could be shifted to a different ratio of small to large squares, or the dimensions of the patio could be changed.

The ground in our site was so firm, dry and compacted that once the formwork was in place, we were able to simply fill the frame with concrete and lay the slabs. But if the ground in your garden is soft, insert a 100 mm layer of hardcore before laying the concrete.

Getting started

Once you have studied your site, draw up a 300 mm grid. If you want to vary the ratios of the three different slab sizes from those we have described, to make a different pattern, play around with the various options to work out how many of each type of slab you need.

You will need

Tools

✔ Tape measure and straight-edge

✔ Pegs and string

✔ Crosscut saw

✔ Spirit level

✔ Claw hammer

✔ Spade, fork and shovel

✔ Wheelbarrow and bucket

✔ Tamping beam: about 1.6 m long, 60 mm wide and 30 mm thick

✔ Club hammer

✔ Soft-bristled brush

✔ Pointing trowel

Materials

For a patio 3 m square

✔ Reconstituted York stone paving:
12 slabs, 600 mm x 600 mm;
18 slabs, 600 mm x 300 mm;
16 slabs, 300 mm x 300 mm

✔ Pine: 5 boards, 3 m long, 150 mm wide and 20 mm thick (formwork)

✔ Pine: 20 battens, 300 mm long, 30 mm wide and 20 mm thick (formwork pegs)

✔ Old boards to use as tread boards

✔ Concrete: 1 part (200 kg) cement, 5 parts (1000 kg) ballast

✔ Mortar: 1 part (20 kg) cement, 3 parts (60 kg) soft sand

✔ Nails: 1 kg of 38 mm-long nails

Overall dimensions and general notes

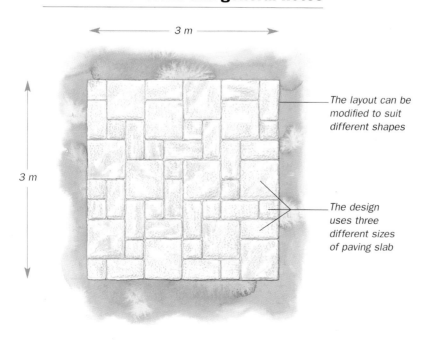

3 m

3 m

The layout can be modified to suit different shapes

The design uses three different sizes of paving slab

This patio will slot into many styles of garden successfully. The slabs are generally sold in three colours: buff, light sand and slate grey – choose a single colour or a mixture.

Cut-away view of the Old English random paving

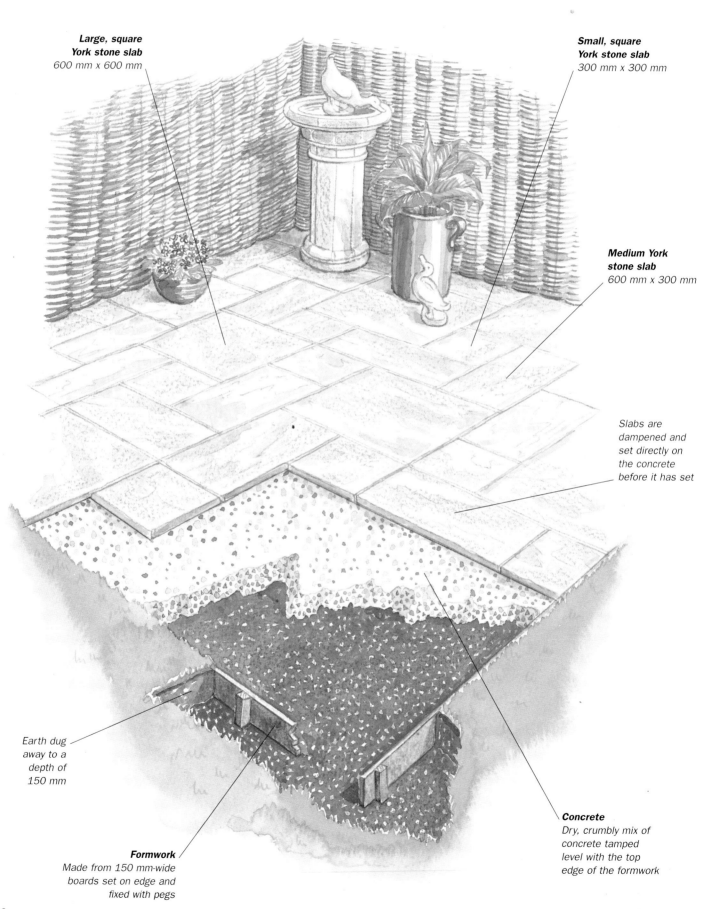

**Large, square
York stone slab**
600 mm x 600 mm

**Small, square
York stone slab**
300 mm x 300 mm

**Medium York
stone slab**
600 mm x 300 mm

*Slabs are
dampened and
set directly on
the concrete
before it has set*

Earth dug
away to a
depth of
150 mm

Formwork
*Made from 150 mm-wide
boards set on edge and
fixed with pegs*

Concrete
*Dry, crumbly mix of
concrete tamped
level with the top
edge of the formwork*

Making the Old English random paving

1 Building the formwork
Measure out the site and set the formwork boards in place – one on each of the four sides, and one down the middle. Level the boards and then adjust them so that there is a slight slope from one side of the site to another (for drainage).

2 Laying the concrete
Fix the formwork boards with formwork pegs and nails. Make a dry, crumbly mix of concrete and spread it over the base of the patio. Use the tamping beam to scrape the concrete level with the top edge of the formwork.

3 Laying the slabs
Dampen the back of the slabs and, very carefully, set them one at a time on the concrete. Use the handle of the club hammer to tap them level to each other.

4 Protecting the slabs
When it is necessary to walk over the slabs, cover them with the tread boards so that your weight is evenly spread, which will prevent the slabs from being knocked out of alignment. Step off the tread boards only when you are laying a slab.

5 Pointing
When the concrete has cured, mix the mortar to a dry, crumbly consistency and use the brush to sweep it between the slabs. Finally, use the pointing trowel to stroke the mortar to a smooth finish. Brush off any excess mortar.

Serpentine path

The serpentine path is a wonderful solution when you want an exciting and dynamic path to wind its way around various features in the garden. Its design also gives you the opportunity to keep your options about the precise shape and route of the path open until the last minute. It has been made from grey slabs throughout, but you could use a different colour, or even a combination of colours, if desired.

Intermediate

Making time
One weekend
One day for preparation, and one day for laying the slabs and making good

Overall dimensions and general notes

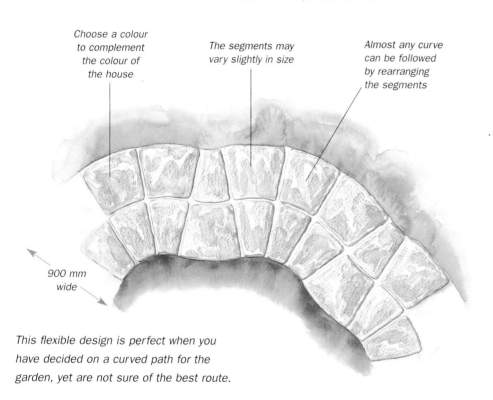

Choose a colour to complement the colour of the house

The segments may vary slightly in size

Almost any curve can be followed by rearranging the segments

900 mm wide

This flexible design is perfect when you have decided on a curved path for the garden, yet are not sure of the best route.

You will need

Tools
- ✔ Tape measure and chalk
- ✔ Spade, fork and shovel
- ✔ Wheelbarrow and bucket
- ✔ Rake and stiff-bristled broom
- ✔ Sledgehammer
- ✔ Bricklayer's trowel
- ✔ Tamping beam: about 1.5 m long, 60 mm wide and 30 mm thick
- ✔ Club hammer

Materials

For 4 m of path, 900 mm wide
- ✔ Middle segment paving slabs (reconstituted stone): 12 slabs, 450 mm radius
- ✔ Outer segment paving slabs (reconstituted stone): 12 slabs, 450 mm radius
- ✔ Sharp sand: about 400 kg
- ✔ Fine gravel: about 300 kg
- ✔ Mortar: 1 part (25 kg) cement, 2 parts (50 kg) soft sand

Considering the design

The path is made up from the middle and outer slabs in a circular patio kit. The slabs are set down in pairs to form two-slab wedges, and alternate wedges are reversed along the course of the path. If you want the path to follow a direct route you reverse every other pair of slabs, whereas if you want it to bend to run around corners, you group the pairs in part-circle curves. The shapes of the slabs allow the path to run around bends and over bumps. Using a combination of middle segment and outer segment paving slabs, both measuring 450 mm on the radius line, the path works out to be about 900 mm wide. Quantities have been given per 4 m of path – adjust to suit your requirements.

Getting started

Take three or four paired slabs and put them on the lawn. Experiment with various arrangements in order to see how to steer the path around both gentle and sharp curves along the proposed route.

Cut-away view of the serpentine path

Outer segment paving slab
Large slab with 450 mm radius

Middle segment
Small slab with 450 mm radius

The slabs are gently tamped down so that they are level with each other and with the surrounding lawn

Mortar
Slabs are set on five bun-sized blobs of mortar

Sand
A 50 mm-thick layer of sand is spread over the gravel and compacted

Gravel
A 50 mm-thick layer of gravel is spread over the earth and compacted

The soil is dug away to a depth of 150 mm

Making the serpentine path

1 Setting out the slabs
Set the paired middle and outer segment slabs in place on the ground. Make a swift sketch so that you know how they relate to each other. Number the slabs with chalk if desired. Slice around the arrangement with the spade and then move the slabs to one side.

2 Clearing the site
Dig up the turf – you (or a neighbour) may be able to use it elsewhere. Dig out the topsoil (to a depth of about 150 mm) by slicing it into manageable squares, and use the spade, fork and wheelbarrow to remove it from the site.

3 Making the foundation
Spread and rake a 50 mm layer of gravel over the earth and use the sledgehammer to stamp it down firmly. Shovel sand over the gravel and spread it out until it forms a layer 50 mm thick.

4 Laying the slabs
Dampen the slabs. Set each slab on five generous blobs of mortar and use the tamping beam and club hammer to tap them level with each other and with the lawn bordering the path.

5 Pointing
When the mortar has set (leave for two or three hours), sweep the rest of the sand into the joints and around the slabs. Repeat this procedure over several days until the joints feel firm.

Dry-stone border wall

The technique of building dry-stone walls has evolved over many thousands of years. There are no concrete foundations or complex planning involved, just a slow and methodical procedure of studying the shapes of the field stones and then fitting them together. If you are planning to build a low raised border in your garden, and have a good source of stone, this project provides an absorbing way of constructing it.

★ ★
Intermediate

Making time
One weekend per
4 m of wall
*Half a day for the
trench; rest of the time
for building the wall*

Considering the design

The wall is three courses high, plus a course of coping stones, and built entirely from salvaged stone. We have used large blocks of rough-cut stone for the primary thick course, thin slices of roof stone to fill in the courses, and square blocks of stone for the coping. The most economical way of tackling the project is to use whatever stone is available and modify your technique accordingly.

Dry-stone walling is straightforward, but it does involve a lot of concentration and co-ordination between hand and eye. First, a trench is dug, which is filled with hardcore. The hardcore is compacted to supply a footing. The first course is laid, consisting of primary stones filled and levelled with secondary stones. Earth is raked down behind the wall, then the second course is set in place.

During construction, you will need to check the horizontal level by eye and make sure that the courses are tilted so that, to a small extent, the wall leans back against the bank of earth. Every half metre or so along the courses, the wall must be stabilized by running extra-long stones back into the earth.

Getting started

Work out how long you want your wall to be, divide it by 4 m and multiply the stated quantities accordingly. Order the stone. Ideally, you need stone that shows one straight edge and two smooth faces.

You will need

Tools

✔ Tape measure and straight-edge
✔ Pegs and string
✔ Spade, fork and shovel
✔ Wheelbarrow and bucket
✔ Sledgehammer
✔ Club hammer
✔ Bricklayer's trowel
✔ Mason's hammer
✔ Bolster chisel
✔ Old carpet: 300 mm x 600 mm

Materials

For 4 m of wall, 550 mm high

✔ Salvaged rough-cut stone:
  ½ cu. m (wall and coping)
✔ Salvaged roof stone:
  1 wheelbarrow load
✔ Hardcore: 12 bucketfuls

Overall dimensions and general notes

4 m long

550 mm
high

This is an ideal project when you want to create a retaining wall for a raised border. The length and height of the wall can be adjusted to suit.

Cut-away view of the dry-stone border wall

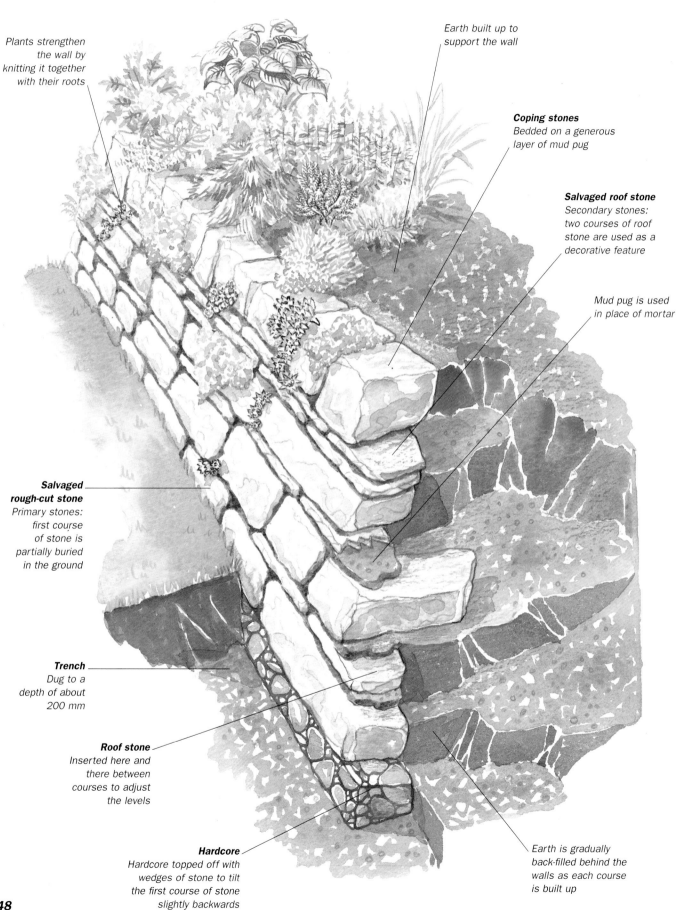

Plants strengthen the wall by knitting it together with their roots

Earth built up to support the wall

Coping stones
Bedded on a generous layer of mud pug

Salvaged roof stone
Secondary stones: two courses of roof stone are used as a decorative feature

Mud pug is used in place of mortar

Salvaged rough-cut stone
Primary stones: first course of stone is partially buried in the ground

Trench
Dug to a depth of about 200 mm

Roof stone
Inserted here and there between courses to adjust the levels

Hardcore
Hardcore topped off with wedges of stone to tilt the first course of stone slightly backwards

Earth is gradually back-filled behind the walls as each course is built up

Making the dry-stone border wall

1 Digging a foundation
Dig away the soil down to ground level to reveal the bank of earth that needs retaining. Excavate a trench 300 mm wide and 200 mm deep, and half-fill it with compacted hardcore.

2 Making mud pug
Take a bucket or so of topsoil and mix it with water until it has the consistency of mortar – this mixture is called mud pug and is used in place of mortar. Remove all the large stones.

3 Laying the first course
Lay the first course of stones on the levelled hardcore, with wedges or slivers of roof stone underneath to ensure that the course is angled slightly backwards. Rake earth down from the bank to back-fill behind the course. Compact the earth with the club hammer.

4 Levelling the course of stone
Use roof stone to bring all the stones of the first course up to the same level. Trowel a generous layer of mud pug over the top of the course and lay the roof stone (trim with the mason's hammer as necessary). Run long stones into the bank to provide extra support.

5 Building further courses
If necessary, use the club hammer and bolster chisel to cut and trim stone, resting it on the old piece of carpet. Trowel mud pug into cavities, and tap misfitting stones back into line. Adjust individual stones by banging small slivers of waste stone into the mud pug.

6 Bedding the coping stones
Continue building the wall until it is three courses high. Now trowel a layer of mud pug over the top course, and bed the coping stones in place.

Japanese rockery

★★
Intermediate

Making time
One weekend
*One day for selecting
the stones, and one
day for building
the rockery*

Traditional Japanese gardens often incorporate a bridge in their design, to symbolize our journey through life. This Japanese-inspired rockery includes a stepping-stone bridge and other symbolic features such as a lantern to represent a guiding light, and shards of weathered plum slate to depict water. If you would like to create an original rockery with a philosophical twist, this project will provide a great talking point.

Overall dimensions and general notes

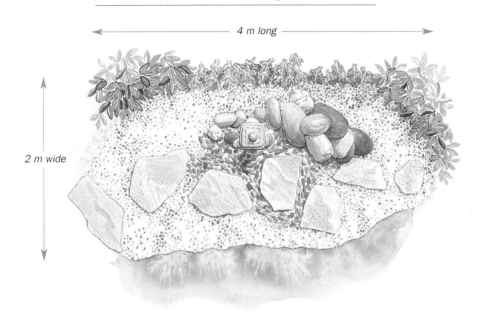

4 m long

2 m wide

This rockery is simply an arrangement of beautiful stones with a hand-built lantern as the central feature, and is suited to any modern garden. The size of the rockery can be adjusted to suit a smaller space. If you prefer, you could use a shop-bought lantern.

You will need

Tools

✔ Tape measure, knife, straight-edge

✔ Pegs and string

✔ Spade, fork, shovel, wheelbarrow, bucket, pointing trowel, spirit level

Materials

For a rockery 4 m long and 2 m wide

✔ Block of salvaged, weathered, cut stone: 400 mm long and 150 mm square (lantern column)

✔ Slab of salvaged, weathered, cut stone: 200 mm square and 50–60 mm thick (lantern table)

✔ Sandstone: 20 pieces, about 50 mm in diameter (lantern pillars)

✔ Slab of salvaged, weathered, cut stone: 150 mm square and 50–60 mm thick (lantern roof)

✔ Large feature stone: about 80 mm in diameter (finial cobble)

✔ Split sandstone: 7 or 8 large slices, about 300–400 mm wide (stepping stones)

✔ Boulders: about 6, ranging in size from 150–400 mm in diameter, in colours and textures to suit ("mountains")

✔ Slate, weathered: 50 kg, plum colour ("water")

✔ Pea gravel: 150 kg ("shore")

✔ Woven plastic sheet: 4 m x 2 m

✔ Mortar: 1 part (2 kg) cement, 1 part (2 kg) lime, 4 parts (8 kg) soft sand

Considering the design

The rockery measures about 4 m long and 2 m wide. It has slate to suggest a turbulent flow of water, fine pea gravel to mark the shore at the water's edge, large sandstone slabs to form a bridge over the water, rocks that resemble mountains and symbolize barriers, and a stone lantern that indicates light, hope and guidance.

You can choose just about any stones that take your fancy for the stepping stones and the "water", but the lantern requires rocks of a certain shape and size.

The main column is 400 mm long and 150 mm square, with 100 mm of its length buried in the ground. The table at the top of the column is 200 mm square, and the lantern roof is 150 mm square.

Getting started

Take a pencil, tape measure and a notebook to the stoneyard, and spend time studying what is on offer. Select stones and rocks for the various components and lay them out on the ground to see how they look together.

Exploded view of the Japanese rockery

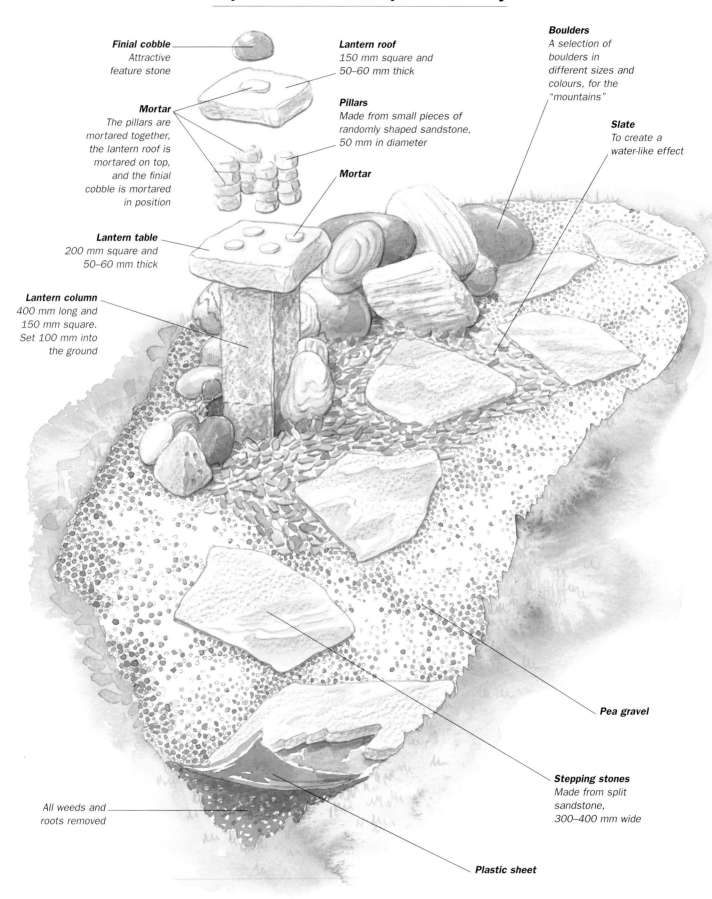

Finial cobble — Attractive feature stone

Lantern roof
150 mm square and 50–60 mm thick

Pillars
Made from small pieces of randomly shaped sandstone, 50 mm in diameter

Boulders
A selection of boulders in different sizes and colours, for the "mountains"

Mortar
The pillars are mortared together, the lantern roof is mortared on top, and the finial cobble is mortared in position

Slate
To create a water-like effect

Mortar

Lantern table
200 mm square and 50–60 mm thick

Lantern column
400 mm long and 150 mm square. Set 100 mm into the ground

Pea gravel

Stepping stones
Made from split sandstone, 300–400 mm wide

All weeds and roots removed

Plastic sheet

Making the Japanese rockery

1 Digging the column hole
Measure out the site and stand the lantern column in the most suitable position. Mark around it with the spade, move the stone and dig a hole to a depth of about 100 mm.

2 Laying the plastic
Spread the plastic sheet over the site and cut a hole in it, aligned with the hole in the ground. Lower the lantern column into the hole and check that it is upright. Fold under the outer edges of the sheet to match the shape of the site.

3 Placing the stones
Start to arrange the rockery stones – the stepping stones for the bridge over the water, and the boulders to act as the mountain range. Consider your use of shape and colour carefully.

5 Finishing
Spread mortar on top of the lantern column and set the table stone in place. Mortar the little sandstones upon each other to make the pillars. Mortar the roof stone and the finial cobble. Spread the rest of the pea gravel over the plastic sheet, making sure it is all covered.

4 Arranging the slate
Spread the plum-coloured slate in and around the stones to suggest a flow of water. Add pea gravel along its borders to create a shore. Take your time, standing back frequently to study the arrangement. Follow your own design instincts.

Stone sett and brick path

The sett and brick path is good on many counts – it makes an excellent footpath, the surface is sturdy enough for a wheelbarrow to be pushed along it, and it is perfect when you want to build a path across a lawn. The flexibility of the flow of bricks neatly does away with the need for a lot of forward planning. Best of all, you can mow straight over the whole path without damaging your lawnmower.

Making time
One weekend
One day for putting down the sand, and one day for laying the setts and bricks

Considering the design

Because of the firm and stony nature of the topsoil in our garden, we were able to lay the path with nothing more than a thick layer of sand as a foundation. However, if your soil is soft and boggy, you need to lay down a layer of gravel or hardcore prior to the sand.

Getting started

The quantities we have given are for a path that is 1 m wide and 3 m long. Study your lawn and consider the route for the path. Measure the length of path required, and then modify the quantities accordingly. Decide what you are going to do with the excavated turf and topsoil.

First of all, have a dry run with the setts and bricks to check the placement. Then remove the turf, compact the earth and put down the sand foundation. Position the bricks, add extra sand where the setts will go, to make up the difference in thickness between bricks and setts, and lay the reconstituted grey stone setts. Push soil into the spaces between the bricks and the setts and sprinkle with grass seed.

You will need

Tools

- ✔ Tape measure and straight-edge
- ✔ Spade, fork and shovel
- ✔ Wheelbarrow and bucket
- ✔ Rake
- ✔ Sledgehammer
- ✔ Bricklayer's trowel
- ✔ Club hammer
- ✔ Tamping beam: about 1.5 m long, 60 mm wide and 30 mm thick
- ✔ Stiff-bristled broom

Materials

For a path 3 m long and 1 m wide

- ✔ Reconstituted paving setts: 112 components 80–100 mm square and 50 mm thick, charcoal colour
- ✔ Bricks: 32 bricks, 225 mm long, 112.5 mm wide and 75 mm thick, colour and texture to suit
- ✔ Sand: about 150 kg
- ✔ Topsoil: about 75 kg
- ✔ Grass seed: about 9 good handfuls
- ✔ Wooden workboards to protect the lawn: size and number to suit your situation

Overall dimensions and general notes

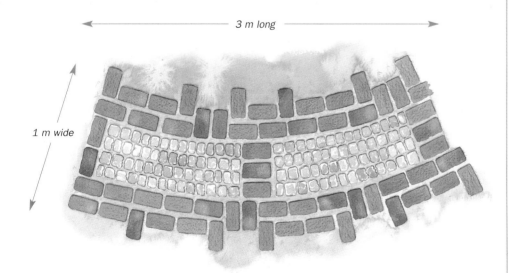

← 3 m long →

1 m wide

A traditional path built from a mixture of bricks and stone setts. It looks especially good in a country garden setting. It is easy to build and does not use any cement, so you can take as much time as you like to lay the bricks and setts.

Cut-away view of the stone sett and brick path

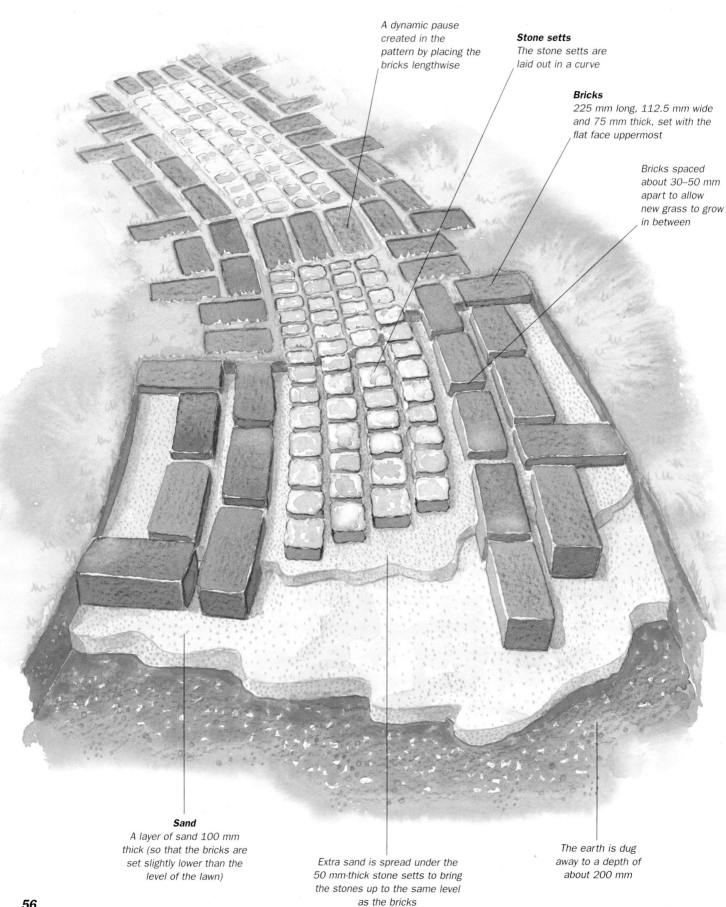

A dynamic pause created in the pattern by placing the bricks lengthwise

Stone setts
The stone setts are laid out in a curve

Bricks
225 mm long, 112.5 mm wide and 75 mm thick, set with the flat face uppermost

Bricks spaced about 30–50 mm apart to allow new grass to grow in between

Sand
A layer of sand 100 mm thick (so that the bricks are set slightly lower than the level of the lawn)

Extra sand is spread under the 50 mm-thick stone setts to bring the stones up to the same level as the bricks

The earth is dug away to a depth of about 200 mm

Making the stone sett and brick path

1 Checking the placement
Position the stone setts on the lawn and arrange the bricks so that there is a uniform spacing of about 30–50 mm between the various components. Make a swift sketch so that you know what goes where.

2 Removing the turf
Slice around the arrangement with the spade. Remove the setts and bricks, and cut the turf into manageable squares. Use the fork and wheelbarrow to remove the turf from the site.

3 Laying the sand
Rake the earth level and compact it with the sledgehammer. Spread a 100 mm-thick layer of sand over the earth and rake it so that it looks more or less level with the surrounding lawn.

4 Positioning the stones
Place the stone setts into position down the middle of the path. Place the bricks on either side of the setts, using uniform spacing of 30–50 mm. With club hammer and beam, tamp them level with each other and a bit lower than the lawn.

5 Finishing
Lay the setts on an extra layer of sand to bring them up level with the bricks and the lawn. Brush the topsoil into the joints, tamp everything level, and sprinkle grass seed in the joints.

Plinth and slab table

This table is a beautifully simple idea – just a single slab of stone set on a low plinth, and is reminiscent of Eastern garden designs. Use it for drinks or for serving afternoon tea. The beauty of this piece of garden furniture is that it is weatherproof, and doesn't have to be taken in at the end of the day. It can also double up as a display plinth, ideal for showing containers of plants or a favourite piece of sculpture.

Making time
One weekend
One day for casting the foundation slab, and one day for building the table

Considering the design

The table is straightforward – it consists of three courses of split sandstone topped off with a massive flagstone, all mounted on a concrete foundation slab. The plinth stands about 300 mm high, and the tabletop is 650 mm x 600 mm.

Visit a stoneyard to obtain materials – the best way to make your choice is to chalk out the 450 mm x 400 mm plan view on the ground, and carefully select enough pieces of 100 mm-thick stone to complete the three courses. Allow one or two extra stones for each course (so you can choose the best fit when you get home) and include twelve good, square-cut corner stones – four for each course. Choose a single flagstone for the table-top, which shows one good face.

Getting started

Select the site and stack the stone so that it is close to hand. Build the formwork, making the interior dimensions 400 mm long and 450 mm wide. Set it in position in your garden. Cut around the frame and remove the turf and earth to a depth of 100 mm. Level the frame in the recess.

You will need

Tools

- ✔ Tape measure, chalk, spirit level
- ✔ Crosscut saw and claw hammer
- ✔ Spade and shovel
- ✔ Tamping beam: 600 mm long, 80 mm wide and 50 mm thick
- ✔ Workboards: planks and pieces of hardboard to protect the area around the site
- ✔ Club hammer and bolster chisel
- ✔ Mason's hammer
- ✔ Bricklayer's and pointing trowels

Materials

For a table 650 mm long, 600 mm wide and 370 mm high

- ✔ Flagstone: 1 salvaged slate/sandstone/limestone flag, 650 mm long, 600 mm wide and 70 mm thick
- ✔ Split sandstone: 1 sq. m of sandstone (pieces about 120–250 mm long, 50–150 mm wide and 100 mm thick)
- ✔ Concrete: 1 part (10 kg) cement, 2 parts (20 kg) sharp sand, 3 parts (30 kg) aggregate
- ✔ Mortar: 2 parts (24 kg) cement, 1 part (12 kg) lime, 9 parts (108 kg) soft sand
- ✔ Pine: 1 piece rough-sawn pine, 2 m long, 80 mm wide and 50 mm thick (formwork)
- ✔ Nails: 4 x 100 mm-long nails

Overall dimensions and general notes

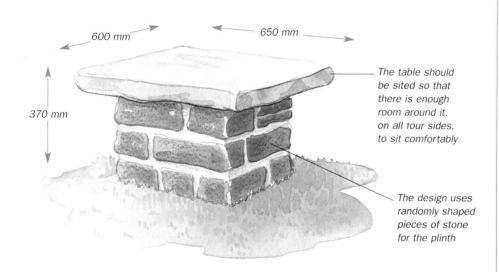

600 mm
650 mm
370 mm

The table should be sited so that there is enough room around it, on all four sides, to sit comfortably

The design uses randomly shaped pieces of stone for the plinth

This timeless design will suit almost any style and size of garden and will last a lifetime. It is constructed from natural stone rather than the reconstituted variety, and so requires a little bit of patience to select and arrange the parts into a pleasing whole.

Exploded view of the plinth and slab table

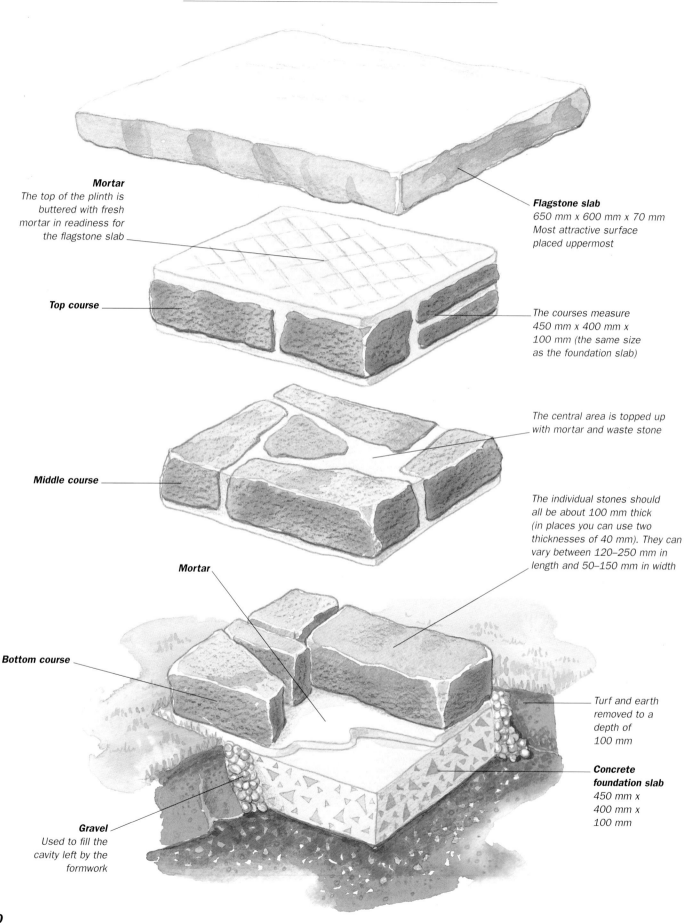

Mortar
The top of the plinth is buttered with fresh mortar in readiness for the flagstone slab

Top course

Middle course

Mortar

Bottom course

Gravel
Used to fill the cavity left by the formwork

Flagstone slab
650 mm x 600 mm x 70 mm
Most attractive surface placed uppermost

The courses measure 450 mm x 400 mm x 100 mm (the same size as the foundation slab)

The central area is topped up with mortar and waste stone

The individual stones should all be about 100 mm thick (in places you can use two thicknesses of 40 mm). They can vary between 120–250 mm in length and 50–150 mm in width

Turf and earth removed to a depth of 100 mm

Concrete foundation slab
450 mm x 400 mm x 100 mm

Making the plinth and slab table

1 Making the frame
Set the wooden formwork frame in the excavation and wedge it level with stones. Check with the spirit level. Fill the frame with concrete. Use the tamping beam to level the concrete with the top edge of the frame. Leave to set. (The formwork is removed later.)

2 Trial layout
Protect the area around the concrete foundation with workboards. Arrange the pieces of stone on the foundation, so that you have all the makings for three 100 mm-high courses. From course to course, make sure the vertical joints are staggered.

3 Breaking stone
To break a piece of stone, set the stone on the grass, position the bolster chisel firmly on the line of cut, and give it one or more well-placed blows with the club hammer. Make sure that you wear goggles and gloves. Use the mason's hammer to trim stone.

4 Laying the first course
Spread a generous layer of mortar over the foundation and lay the first course of stones. Use the weight of the club hammer to gently tap the stones level. Check with the spirit level.

5 Second and third courses
Repeat the procedure to build the other two courses. Fill the central area of the plinth with a mixture of mortar and fragments of waste stone. Use the pointing trowel to tidy up the mortar in the joints of the courses.

6 Laying the flagstone
When you have achieved a level, square pillar, spread a generous layer of fresh mortar over the top of the stack. Dampen the underside of the flagstone slab and get help to gently lower it into position. Pour gravel into the slot between the plinth and the grass.

Boulder and coping wall

This little wall is charming in its simplicity and directness. You don't have to engage in a lot of forward planning – you simply order a heap of random split sandstone and a limestone boulder for every metre of wall, and start building. The more challenging part is building the scalloped coping, but it is great fun to do. An added advantage is that the modest weight of the components means that the project is open to everyone.

★ ★
Intermediate

Making time
One weekend for every 3 m of wall
One day for building the basic wall, and one day for the coping

Overall dimensions and general notes

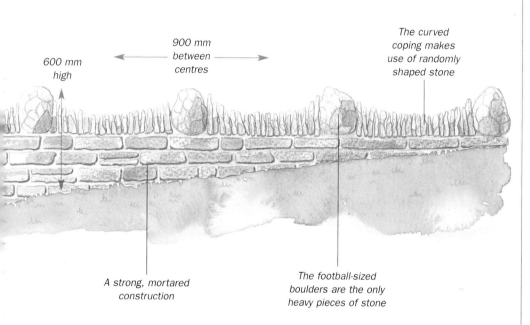

900 mm between centres

600 mm high

The curved coping makes use of randomly shaped stone

A strong, mortared construction

The football-sized boulders are the only heavy pieces of stone

The project produces a low, decorative wall. It is perfect for creating a raised bed – simply build end walls, fill with a layer of gravel for drainage, top with soil and plant up.

You will need

Tools
✔ Tape measure
✔ Pegs and string
✔ Spade, fork and shovel
✔ Wheelbarrow and bucket
✔ Sledgehammer
✔ Bricklayer's trowel
✔ Club hammer
✔ Mason's hammer
✔ Pointing trowel
✔ Old hand brush

Materials
For 1 m of wall, 600 mm high

✔ Sandstone: about 2 wheelbarrow loads of random stones in various sizes and thicknesses

✔ Limestone boulder: 1 large, football-sized stone

✔ Hardcore (waste stone): 9 bucketfuls

✔ Mortar: 1 part (25 kg) cement, 3 parts (75 kg) soft sand

Considering the design

The wall is built up from just below ground level, with the first course of stone set on a layer of compacted waste stone. First you dig a shallow trench, stamp all the bits of waste stone into the bottom of it with a sledgehammer, and then set the first course in the trench so that it is just below ground level.

When the wall is about three or four courses high, the top of the wall is buttered with a generous wedge of mortar, and the boulder and stone slices for the coping are set in place. All you do is mark in the position of the boulders, and the halfway point between them. Then set the first boulder in place and arrange the coping so that the pieces descend in size up to the midway point, and then increase in size up to the next boulder.

Getting started

Work out how long you want your wall to be. The quantities given are per 1 m of wall: multiply as necessary. Visit the stoneyard, discuss what you are planning to build, and choose some attractive boulders and random split sandstone.

Cut-away view of the boulder and coping wall

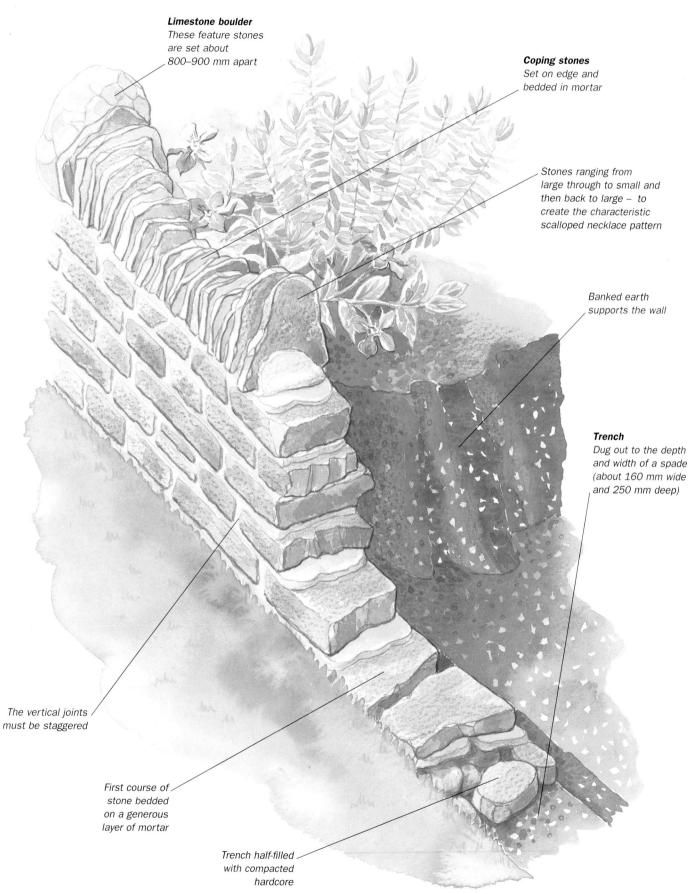

Limestone boulder
These feature stones are set about 800–900 mm apart

Coping stones
Set on edge and bedded in mortar

Stones ranging from large through to small and then back to large – to create the characteristic scalloped necklace pattern

Banked earth supports the wall

Trench
Dug out to the depth and width of a spade (about 160 mm wide and 250 mm deep)

The vertical joints must be staggered

First course of stone bedded on a generous layer of mortar

Trench half-filled with compacted hardcore

Making the boulder and coping wall

1 Marking out
Use the string and pegs to mark out the dimensions of the wall. Dig a trench to the depth and width of a spade (about 160 mm wide and 250 mm deep). Half-fill the trench with hardcore and compact it with the sledgehammer.

2 Laying the first course
Trowel a generous layer of mortar into the trench and set the first course of stone in place. Level up by eye and use the club hammer to make adjustments. Rake earth up behind the inside face of the wall to support it.

3 Adding more courses
Continue building one course upon another, all the while doing your best to ensure that the vertical joints are staggered. Fill the cavities with mortar and slivers of sandstone.

4 Placing the boulders
Generously butter the top of the wall with mortar. Mark the positions of the boulders and halfway points between them. Place the first boulder, and then range slices of stone on edge, running in a scallop pattern to the next boulder. Use the mason's hammer to trim stones.

5 Pointing
Finally, use the pointing trowel to fill the joints with mortar. Sculpt the topmost wedge of mortar, between the coping stones and the rest of the wall, so that it angles down from the coping. Tidy up the joints and brush off surplus mortar.

Inlay block steps

This is the ideal project for a minimalist. If you have a crisp, modern home with lots of glass and concrete painted in flat colours, inlay block steps in the garden will complement it perfectly. This simple flight of steps can be built with the minimum of fuss. Each step is decorated with a small amount of detailing, made up of slivers of Welsh slate arranged in an attractive basketweave pattern.

Making time
One weekend
One day for getting the flight of steps into place; one day for the detailing and finishing

Considering the design

Each step consists of two hollow concrete blocks, making a 440 mm square. The whole flight is dug into the ground and the top step is flush with ground level. This technique negates the need both for complex measuring and for side retaining walls. Each step stands clear and separate from its neighbour. Once the blocks are in place, the hollows in them are filled with concrete, topped with mortar and studded with stone, both for decorative effect and to provide a firm footing.

Getting started

Once you have taken delivery of the blocks, play around with various arrangements until you have a clear picture of how they relate to each other. Make a sketch and take measurements.

Overall dimensions and general notes

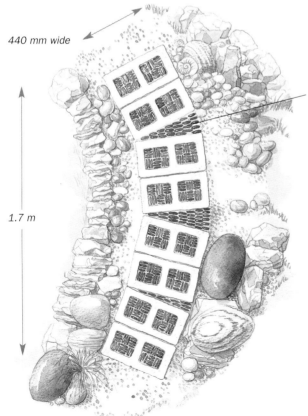

440 mm wide

The angles between the steps can be adjusted to suit almost any curve

1.7 m

These steps draw their inspiration from an architect-designed building by the sea. They are particularly easy to build and can be painted in whatever colours you wish.

You will need

Tools

- ✔ Tape measure and straight-edge
- ✔ Pegs and string
- ✔ Spade, fork and shovel
- ✔ Spirit levels: one long and one short
- ✔ Wheelbarrow and bucket
- ✔ Bricklayer's trowel
- ✔ Pointing trowel
- ✔ Soft-bristled brush
- ✔ Paintbrush

Materials

For a flight of steps about 1.7 m long and 440 mm wide

- ✔ Hollow concrete building blocks: 8 blocks, 440 mm long, 210 mm wide and 210 mm thick
- ✔ Welsh plum slate: 25 kg
- ✔ Rocks and cobbles: 2 wheelbarrow loads (to decorate the site)
- ✔ Concrete: 1 part (20 kg) cement, 5 parts (100 kg) ballast
- ✔ Mortar: 1 part (10 kg) cement, 2 parts (20 kg) soft sand
- ✔ Paint: exterior-grade flat paint in colour to suit

Exploded view of the inlay block steps

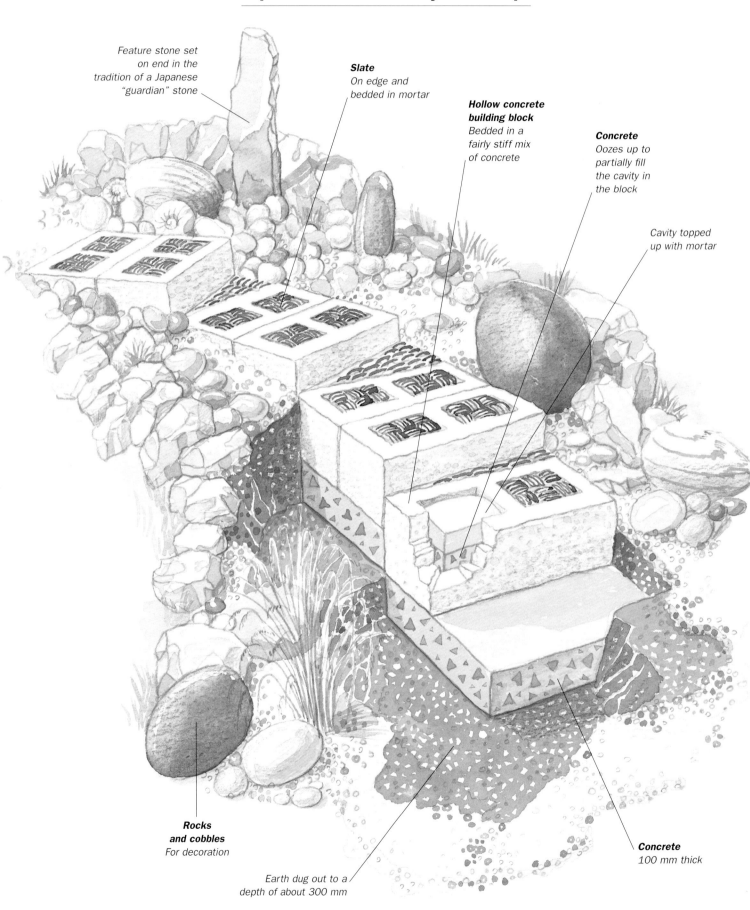

Feature stone set on end in the tradition of a Japanese "guardian" stone

Slate
On edge and bedded in mortar

Hollow concrete building block
Bedded in a fairly stiff mix of concrete

Concrete
Oozes up to partially fill the cavity in the block

Cavity topped up with mortar

Rocks and cobbles
For decoration

Earth dug out to a depth of about 300 mm

Concrete
100 mm thick

Making the inlay block steps

1 Trial arrangement
Arrange the concrete blocks in pairs along the proposed route of the path, so that each pair stands separate, and so that the total flight gradually angles to follow the route.

2 Clearing the turf
Use the spade to mark around the pairs of blocks. Remove the blocks, slice away the turf and dig individual holes to a depth of about 300 mm. Use the small spirit level to check that the bottom of the holes are level.

3 Laying the concrete blocks
Make a fairly stiff mix of concrete, spread a 100 mm-thick layer in the bottom of each hole, and set the paired blocks in place. A little concrete will ooze into the cavities. Make adjustments until the blocks are level with each other, and with the whole flight.

4 Step inlays
Trowel concrete into the cavities in the blocks, half-filling them, then add mortar to within 10 mm of the top. Set the Welsh plum slate in the mortar, forming a basketweave pattern. Check that the surface is flush with the block.

5 Painting and decoration
Brush all dust and debris from the blocks, and paint them in your chosen colour. Finally, decorate the site with rocks and cobbles.

Trough planter

★ ★ ★
Advanced

Making time
One weekend
One day for laying the foundation slab, and one day for building the walls

This planter draws its inspiration from the carved stone water troughs seen in fields in northern England. It is made from three courses of reconstituted York stone, and the top of the planter is finished with a traditional coping technique known as "spotted dick" – no doubt named after the steamed pudding popular in that part of the world. This is a good project for a formal garden.

Considering the design

Each course is made up of nine blocks, one of which has to be cut approximately two-thirds of the way along its length (it is pre-marked with registration grooves, scored round the block with a club hammer and bolster chisel). Building the coping is good fun. A generous wedge of mortar is spread on top of the finished trough, modelled to a smooth, half-round section, and then studded with small pebbles.

Getting started

Decide how long you want your trough to be. Have a trial run with the blocks so you know how the courses fit together.

Overall dimensions and general notes

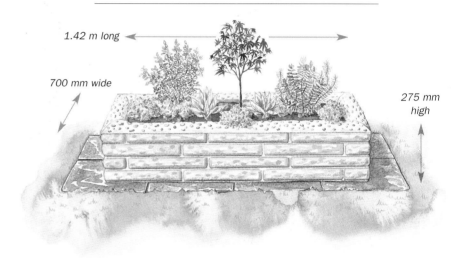

1.42 m long

700 mm wide

275 mm high

A small trough made from reconstituted stone blocks is ideal for a tiny garden. The size of the trough can be adjusted easily, and square or L-shaped configurations are possible.

You will need

Tools

- ✔ Tape measure, straight-edge and chalk
- ✔ Pegs and string
- ✔ Boards to protect the surrounding grass
- ✔ Spade, rake and shovel
- ✔ Wheelbarrow and bucket
- ✔ Crosscut saw
- ✔ Claw hammer
- ✔ Spirit level
- ✔ Sledgehammer

- ✔ Tamping beam: about 1 m long, 60 mm wide and 30 mm thick
- ✔ Bricklayer's trowel
- ✔ Club hammer
- ✔ Bolster chisel
- ✔ Pointing trowel
- ✔ Wire brush
- ✔ Soft-bristled brush

Materials

For a trough 1.42 m long, 700 mm wide and 275 mm high

- ✔ Reconstituted York stone blocks: 36 blocks, 420 mm long, 130 mm wide and 60 mm thick
- ✔ Concrete slabs: 8 slabs, 450 mm square, colour and texture to suit
- ✔ Pebbles: 1 bucketful, size and colour to suit
- ✔ Hardcore: 2 wheelbarrow loads
- ✔ Soft sand: 6 wheelbarrow loads
- ✔ Mortar: 1 part (30 kg) cement, 6 parts (180 kg) soft sand
- ✔ Pine: 6 m long, 75 mm wide and 25 mm thick (formwork)
- ✔ Nails: 1 kg of 38 mm-long nails

Exploded view of the trough planter

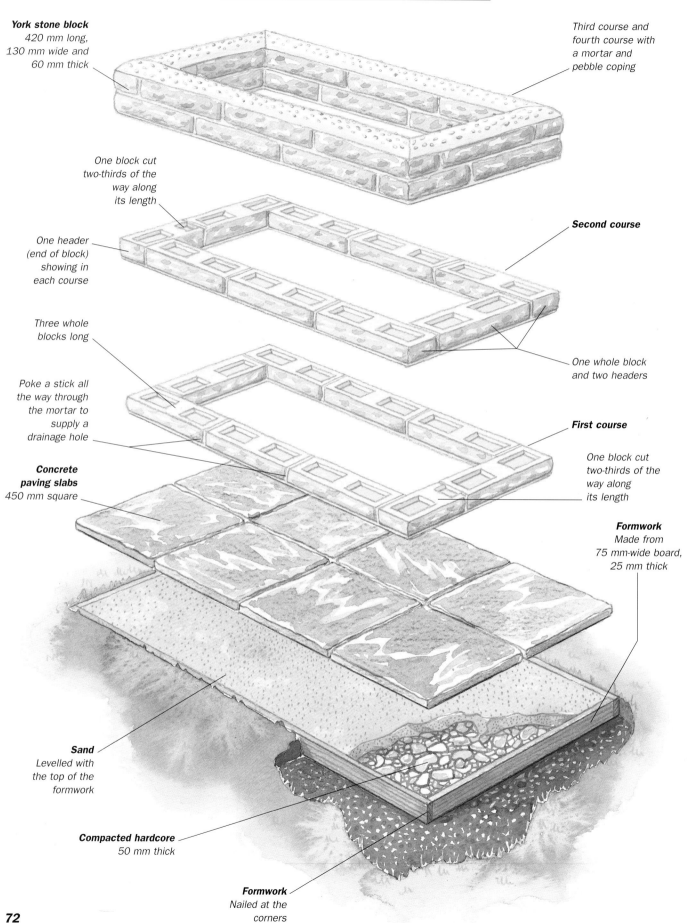

York stone block
420 mm long, 130 mm wide and 60 mm thick

Third course and fourth course with a mortar and pebble coping

One block cut two-thirds of the way along its length

Second course

One header (end of block) showing in each course

Three whole blocks long

One whole block and two headers

Poke a stick all the way through the mortar to supply a drainage hole

First course

One block cut two-thirds of the way along its length

Concrete paving slabs
450 mm square

Formwork
Made from 75 mm-wide board, 25 mm thick

Sand
Levelled with the top of the formwork

Compacted hardcore
50 mm thick

Formwork
Nailed at the corners

Cut-away view of the trough planter

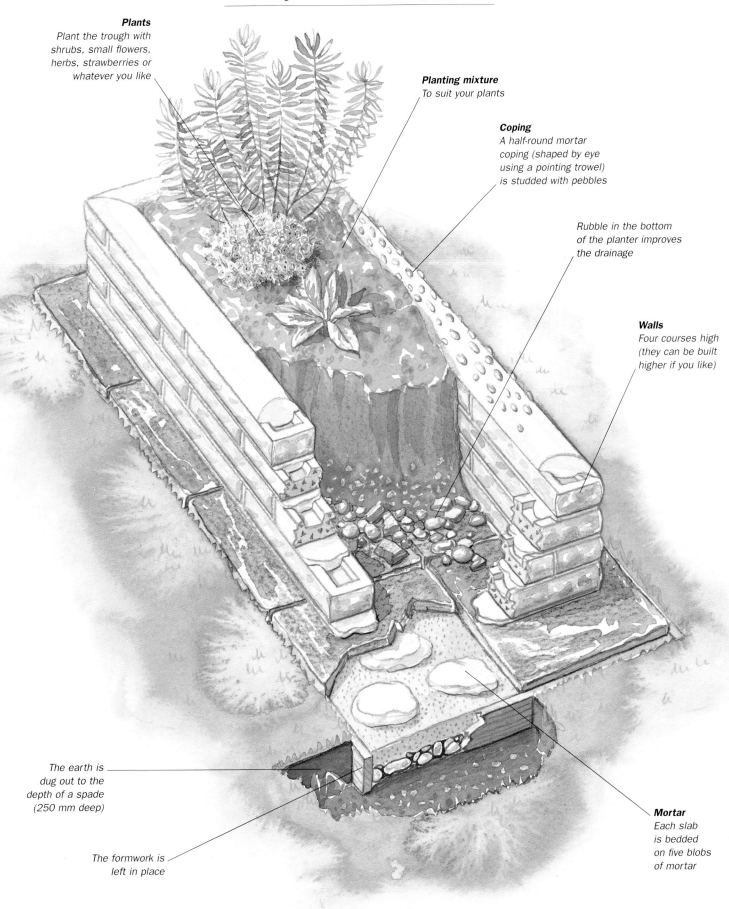

Plants
Plant the trough with shrubs, small flowers, herbs, strawberries or whatever you like

Planting mixture
To suit your plants

Coping
A half-round mortar coping (shaped by eye using a pointing trowel) is studded with pebbles

Rubble in the bottom of the planter improves the drainage

Walls
Four courses high (they can be built higher if you like)

The earth is dug out to the depth of a spade (250 mm deep)

The formwork is left in place

Mortar
Each slab is bedded on five blobs of mortar

Making the trough planter

1 Formwork
Measure out the foundation area, making it 900 mm wide and 1.8 m long. Dig out the area to the depth of the spade. Insert and level the formwork, and fix it in place with nails. Spread hardcore in the formwork frame and compact it with the sledgehammer.

2 Spreading the sand
Shovel sand over the hardcore within the frame and rake it out. Use the tamping beam to compact and level the sand. It should end up as a firm foundation, which is level with the top edge of the formwork.

3 Making the concrete slab base
Mix the mortar to a smooth, firm consistency. Put five generous, bun-shaped blobs on the sand where the first concrete slab will be positioned. Dampen the back of the slab and set it carefully in place upon the sand. Repeat with the other slabs.

4 Laying the first course
Use the tape measure, straight-edge and chalk to set out the shape of the planter on the concrete slab base. Have a dry run to place the first course of York stone blocks. Using club hammer and bolster chisel, cut one block to fit. Check that all is correct.

5 Levelling the blocks
Trowel mortar on the concrete slabs, dampen the blocks for the first course and set them in place. Use the tamping beam, club hammer and spirit level to ensure that the whole course is level. Insert two drainage holes in the mortar as shown on page 72.

6 Building the other courses
Repeat the procedure to build the other three courses. Make sure that all the joints are full of mortar, but at this stage, do not bother to remove the excess. Keep checking that a course is level before building the next course.

7 Checking with the spirit level
When all four courses are in place, use the tamping beam and spirit level to ensure that the horizontal and vertical levels are true. Tap non-aligned blocks into line with the club hammer.

8 Studding with pebbles
With the pointing trowel, lay a generous coping of mortar on the top course and sculpt it to a smooth, half-rounded finish. Press pebbles into the mortar. Use the trowel, wire brush and soft-bristled brush to create a good finish on the courses.

Bench with arch detail

This bench is a beautifully dynamic shape, and the building procedure is very satisfying. When you have run the stone over the formwork, and then removed the formwork to see that the arch actually stands unsupported, it's a triumphal moment. If you had planned to build a bench in your garden, to sit on or perhaps to use as a table, try this project – you will amaze yourself and your friends with your stoneworking skills.

Making time
Two weekends
One day for building the basic arch, and three days for the walls and slabs

Considering the design

The bench is constructed on a base slab (or an existing patio slab). Two pillars are built and plywood sprung between them. Thin slivers of stone are worked into mortar over the plywood, the end and side walls are built up to square off the structure, and finally the structure is topped with slabs to create the seat.

Getting started

Start by searching out the stone. You need a small number of square-edged blocks for the two pillars, and a heap of thin, broken sandstone for the arch.

Overall dimensions and general notes

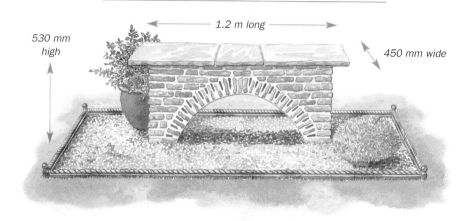

530 mm high

1.2 m long

450 mm wide

This decorative bench has been built on a specially constructed foundation slab, but can be built directly on to an existing patio. The arch is deceptively easy to make.

You will need

Tools

- ✔ Tape measure, chalk and straight-edge
- ✔ Pegs and string
- ✔ Shovel
- ✔ Wheelbarrow and bucket
- ✔ Old carpet: about 300 mm x 600 mm
- ✔ Club hammer
- ✔ Bolster chisel
- ✔ Mason's hammer
- ✔ Bricklayer's trowel
- ✔ Pointing trowel
- ✔ Spirit level
- ✔ Soft-bristled brush

Materials

For a bench 1.2 m long, 450 mm wide and 530 mm high

- ✔ Sandstone: 1 wheelbarrow load of pieces about 150 mm wide and 60–70 mm thick (pillars)
- ✔ Sandstone or salvaged roof stone: 3 wheelbarrow loads of thin split stone (arch and walls)
- ✔ Waste roof stone and broken tiles: 1 bucketful of each (arch)
- ✔ Natural or reconstituted York stone: 2 slabs, 450 mm square; 1 slab, 450 mm long and 300 mm wide (seat)
- ✔ Rope-top edging: 12 edging components, 600 mm long, 150 mm high and 50 mm thick, terracotta colour (to frame the slate infill)

- ✔ Pillar and ball posts: 4 posts, 280 mm high and 60 mm square, terracotta colour (to link the edging)
- ✔ Welsh plum slate chippings: 50 kg (decorative infill)
- ✔ Concrete blocks: 6 blocks, 450 mm long, 225 mm wide and 100 mm thick (for springing the plywood)
- ✔ Formwork or former: a sheet of thin plywood, 900 mm long, 360 mm wide and 5 mm thick (the grain must run across the width of the plywood)
- ✔ Hardcore: 8 wheelbarrow loads
- ✔ Concrete: 1 part (35 kg) cement, 2 parts (70 kg) sharp sand, 3 parts (105 kg) aggregate
- ✔ Mortar: 1 part (25 kg) cement, 3 parts (75 kg) soft sand

Exploded view of the bench with arch detail

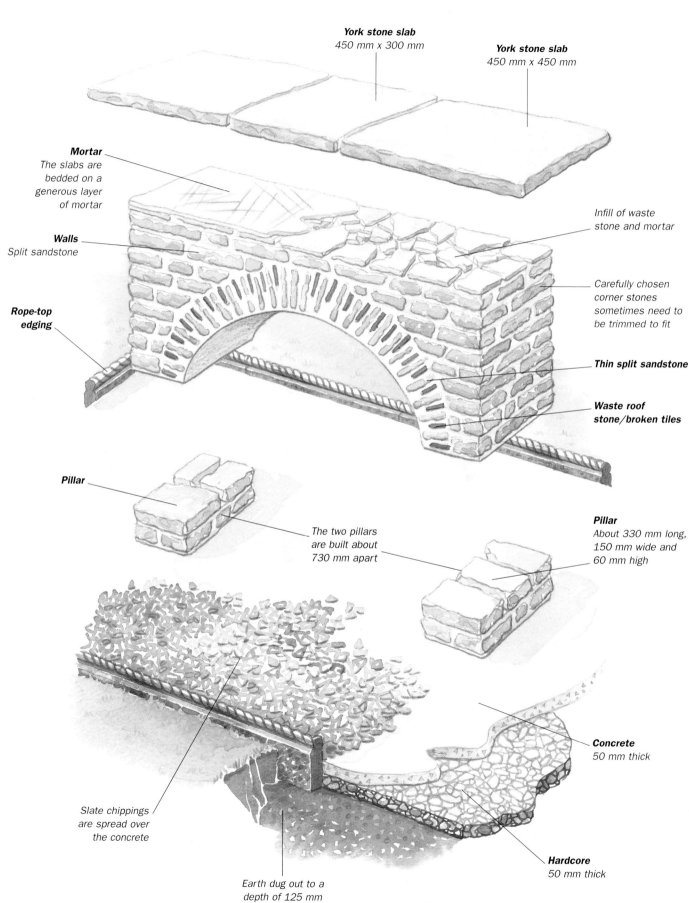

York stone slab
450 mm x 300 mm

York stone slab
450 mm x 450 mm

Mortar
The slabs are bedded on a generous layer of mortar

Infill of waste stone and mortar

Walls
Split sandstone

Carefully chosen corner stones sometimes need to be trimmed to fit

Rope-top edging

Thin split sandstone

Waste roof stone/broken tiles

Pillar

The two pillars are built about 730 mm apart

Pillar
About 330 mm long, 150 mm wide and 60 mm high

Slate chippings are spread over the concrete

Concrete
50 mm thick

Hardcore
50 mm thick

Earth dug out to a depth of 125 mm

Detail of the base of the bench

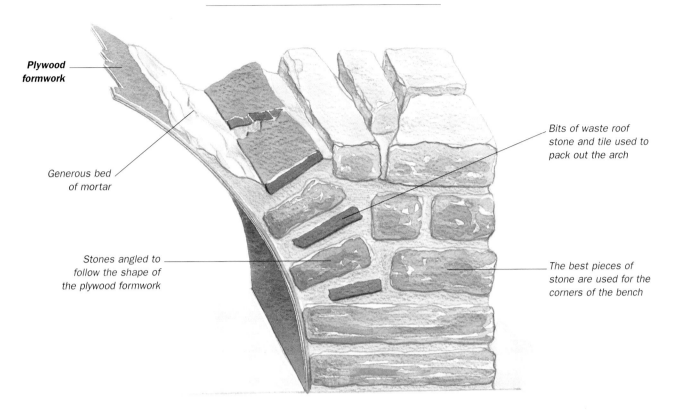

Plywood formwork

Generous bed of mortar

Stones angled to follow the shape of the plywood formwork

Bits of waste roof stone and tile used to pack out the arch

The best pieces of stone are used for the corners of the bench

Cross-section of the bench

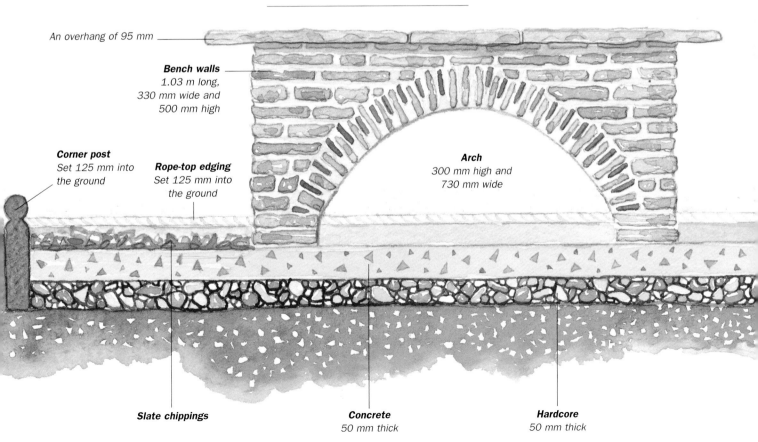

An overhang of 95 mm

Bench walls
1.03 m long, 330 mm wide and 500 mm high

Corner post
Set 125 mm into the ground

Rope-top edging
Set 125 mm into the ground

Arch
300 mm high and 730 mm wide

Slate chippings

Concrete
50 mm thick

Hardcore
50 mm thick

Making the bench with arch detail

1 Measuring out
Build a concrete base slab if needed. Dig out the earth to a depth of 125 mm and compact 50 mm of hardcore in the recess. Lay the concrete. Mark out the seat. The pillars need to measure about 330 mm long x 150 mm wide x 60 mm high, and stand about 730 mm apart.

2 Building the pillars
Build up the two pillars dry, making sure that the corners are, as near as possible, at right angles. Cut stone with the club hammer and bolster chisel, and trim it with the mason's hammer. Then build the pillars with mortar and leave to set for a few hours.

3 Arch formwork
Set the concrete blocks around the pillars and spring the sheet of plywood into an arch, so that it is supported by the concrete blocks and is just touching the inside of the pillars.

5 Removing the plywood
When the mortar has set, carefully remove the plywood and the concrete blocks. Lay courses of stone on the pillars, doing your best to ensure that the corners are crisp and square.

4 Making the arch
Mix the mortar to a soft, buttery consistency and lay the thin pieces of stone over the formwork. Work up from both sides in order to keep the weight equally distributed. Try to keep the sides of the arch aligned with the edge of the plywood.

6 Checking the structure

Every now and again as you are building the walls, stop and use the spirit level to ensure that the sides of the structure are vertically true. Use a hammer or the handle of the trowel to nudge stones into line.

7 Tidying the mortar

Wait until the mortar is crisp (after about two or three hours), and then use the end of the pointing trowel to scrape out excess mortar and reveal the edges of the stones to best advantage, giving the bench a more attractive appearance.

8 Bedding the slabs

Spread a generous layer of mortar over the top of the last course, dampen the back of the seat slabs and gently bed them in place. Make checks with the spirit level and if necessary, tamp the slabs level with the handle of the club hammer.

9 Inserting the rope-top edging

Dig a shallow trench around the base slab and set the rope-top edging and pillar and ball posts in place on a bed of mortar. Check the levels with the spirit level. Tidy up the bench with the brush. Finally, fill the area around the bench with slate chippings.

Crazy-paving steps

If you want a low-cost flight of three or four steps, how about making stone crazy-paving steps? The design harks back to the 1920s, and uses a mixture of natural split sandstone and salvaged cut stone. The low risers make the steps easy to use for everyone, from the very young to older members of the family. The slightly rippled surface of the steps feels good underfoot and is attractive to look at.

Making time
Two weekends
One day for putting in the concrete foundation slab, and three days for building

Considering the design

The steps spring off a single concrete strip foundation slab that runs under the whole flight. The foundation slab is built first, then the first riser, side and back walls. The walls are back-filled with concrete and topped with the crazy paving to make the first tread. Then the next riser wall and related walls are built, back-filled and so on. We have used random split sandstone for the walls, but you could use limestone, or even a mixture of bricks and stone instead: it really depends on your budget and the availability of materials. The height of the riser walls and the depth of the treads are, to a great extent, governed by safety and comfort – low risers are both comfortable and safe to negotiate; however the width of the flight can be shaped to suit the size of your site and your own requirements.

Getting started

Decide how long you want the flight of steps to be. Establish the position and mark out the shape of the foundation slab. Plan how to move around the garden while the steps are being built.

You will need

Tools

✔ Tape measure and straight-edge
✔ Pegs and string
✔ Spade, fork and shovel
✔ Sledgehammer
✔ Wheelbarrow and bucket
✔ Tamping beam: about 1.5 m long, 60 mm wide and 30 mm thick
✔ Club hammer and claw hammer
✔ Mason's hammer
✔ Bricklayer's and pointing trowels
✔ Spirit level
✔ Soft-bristled brush

Materials

For two steps, each 1 m wide, 600 mm deep and 185 mm high

✔ Sandstone: about 1.2 sq. m split stone in random sizes and thicknesses (amount allows for wastage and choice)
✔ Hardcore (builder's rubble or waste stone): about 10 wheelbarrow loads
✔ Pine: 8 m long, 60 mm wide and 30 mm thick (formwork)
✔ Concrete: 1 part (100 kg) cement, 5 parts (500 kg) ballast
✔ Mortar: 1 part (50 kg) cement, 3 parts (150 kg) soft sand (allows for wastage)
✔ Nails: 12 x 50 mm long

Overall dimensions and general notes

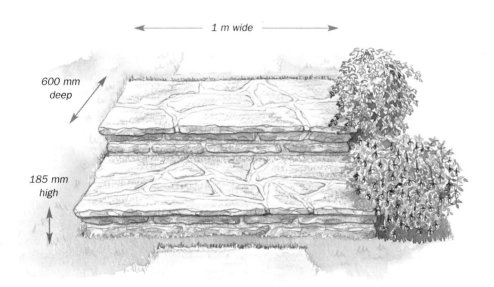

1 m wide

600 mm deep

185 mm high

A good project for a country or urban garden. The crazy paving is an attractive and practical surface for steps (it provides a lot of grip). The width, height and depth of the steps can be adjusted to suit your requirements and the slope of the site.

Exploded view of the crazy-paving steps

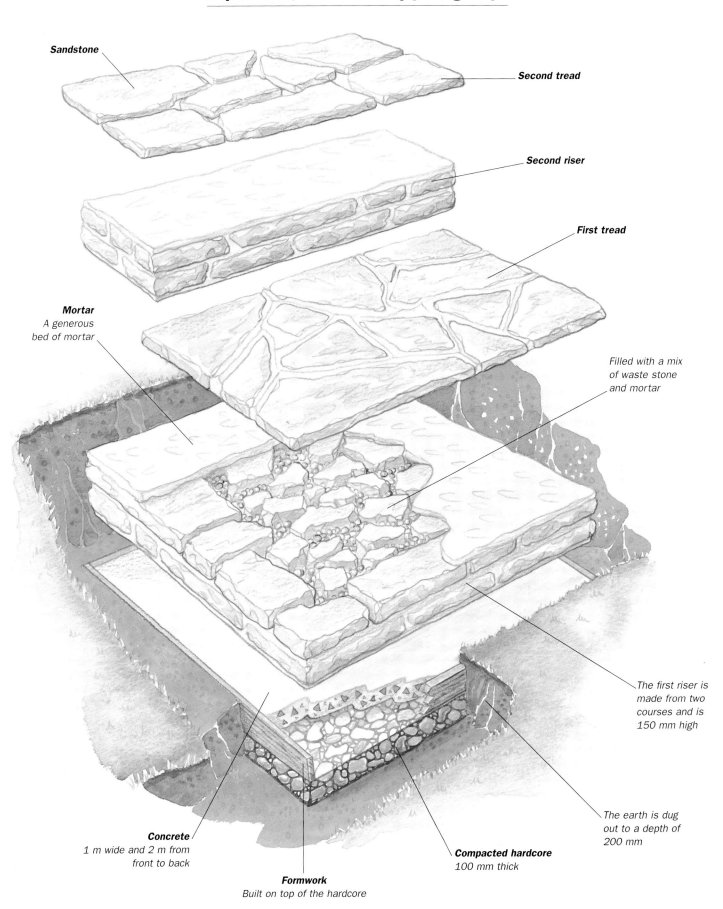

Sandstone

Second tread

Second riser

First tread

Mortar
*A generous
bed of mortar*

*Filled with a mix
of waste stone
and mortar*

*The first riser is
made from two
courses and is
150 mm high*

*The earth is dug
out to a depth of
200 mm*

Concrete
*1 m wide and 2 m from
front to back*

Formwork
Built on top of the hardcore

Compacted hardcore
100 mm thick

Cut-away view of the crazy-paving steps

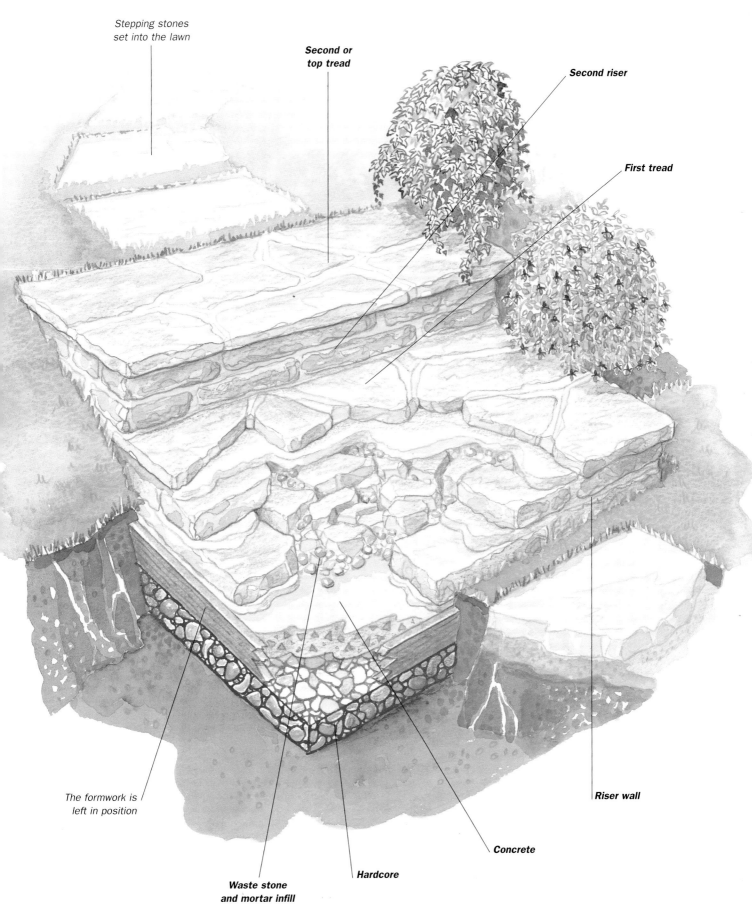

Stepping stones
set into the lawn

Second or
top tread

Second riser

First tread

The formwork is
left in position

Riser wall

Concrete

Hardcore

Waste stone
and mortar infill

Making the crazy-paving steps

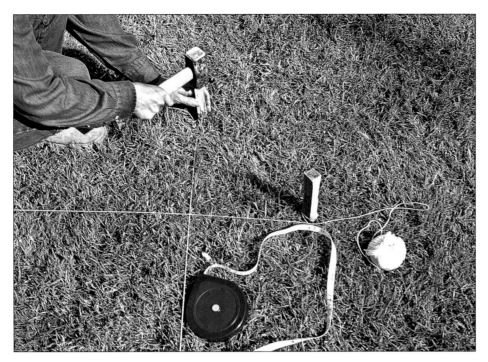

1 Marking out
Use the tape measure, pegs and string to mark out the overall size and shape of the foundation slab, which is 1 m wide and 2 m from front to back. Remove the turf, in squares, from the site (use elsewhere in the garden or give to a friend).

2 Making the foundation slab
Dig out the earth to a depth of 200 mm. Half-fill the recess with hardcore and compact it with the sledgehammer. Fix the formwork and fit it into place. Top the hardcore with a 100 mm-thick layer of concrete, levelling it with the tamping beam.

3 Setting out the first step
Use the tape measure, straight-edge and chalk to set out the position of the first riser wall, side and back walls on the concrete slab. Select stones and lay them out dry. The border is 300 mm wide. Make joints as small as possible and use right-angled stones for corners.

4 Building the first step
Mix the mortar to a buttery consistency and build the riser wall, side and back walls to a height of 150 mm. Back-fill the area within the walls with 125 mm of waste stone and leftover mortar. Top the central area with concrete and level off.

5 Bedding the crazy paving

When the concrete has set, select stones for the crazy paving and lay them on top. Trowel mortar on the concrete and bed the crazy paving in place. Arrange the stones so that there is an overhang to the tread of about 20 mm at the front and side edges.

6 Building the other steps

Measure back 600 mm from the edge of the tread, establishing the depth of the tread and the position of the riser wall for the next step. Repeat the procedure already described to build the next step. Keep checking that everything is level.

7 Selecting crazy paving

When selecting pieces of stone, place them together in different ways to achieve the best fit and reduce the need for cutting. Use the mason's hammer to cut stone. Make up a complete rectangle, the correct size for one tread, before mortaring.

8 Pointing

Use the pointing trowel and some freshly mixed mortar to tool all the courses to an angled finish. Finally, fill the joints between the crazy paving with mortar and work to a peaked finish.

Roman arch shrine

Many countries have an ancient tradition of building shrines in quiet corners of the house and garden, perhaps for religious purposes or for displaying a meaningful family item. This shrine has been inspired by the little arch-topped alcoves and niches common in Italy. It would be perfect for displaying a piece of garden sculpture or a favourite container plant, or it could comprise part of a water feature.

Making time
One weekend
One day for the base slab and formwork, and one day for building the arch

Considering the design

The arch is constructed over a wooden former set on wedges on the base slab, with its back against a wall. Stone is set in mortar over the former, the courses are jointed, and when the mortar has set, the wedges and former are removed. The rule of thumb is the thinner and more uniform the pieces of stone, the easier it is to run them over the arch.

Getting started

Start by building the former. It's very simple – just two sheets of plywood held apart with lengths of wood, and the sides of the shape covered in plywood.

Overall dimensions and general notes

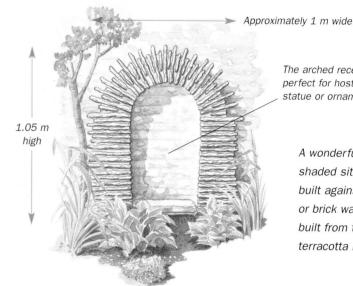

Approximately 1 m wide

1.05 m high

The arched recess is perfect for hosting a statue or ornament

A wonderful project for a shaded site. It needs to be built against an existing stone or brick wall. The arch can be built from thin stone, slate or terracotta roof tiles.

You will need

Tools

✔ Tape measure, straight-edge and compass
✔ Crosscut saw
✔ Electric jigsaw
✔ Claw hammer
✔ Screwdriver
✔ Pegs and string
✔ Spade and shovel
✔ Wheelbarrow and bucket
✔ Spirit level
✔ Sledgehammer
✔ Mason's hammer
✔ Bricklayer's trowel

✔ Pointing trowel
✔ Pliers
✔ Soft-bristled brush

Materials

For an arch 1.05 m high and 1 m wide

✔ Hardcore: about 1 wheelbarrow load
✔ Stone base slab: approx. 1 m long, 300 mm wide and 50 mm thick, colour and texture to suit
✔ Stone plinth slab: approx. 400 mm long, 150 mm wide and 75 mm thick, slightly bigger than the base of the former

✔ Roof stone: 2 wheelbarrow loads of thin stone, either salvaged or split
✔ Plywood: 2 pieces, 700 mm long, 400 mm wide and 4 mm thick; 1 piece, 2 m long, 200 mm wide and 4 mm thick (former)
✔ Pine: 15 pieces, 200 mm long, 35 mm wide and 20 mm thick (former joining battens and wedges)
✔ Mortar: 1 part (10 kg) cement, 1 part (10 kg) lime, 2 parts (20 kg) soft sand
✔ Screws: 50 x 25 mm-long cross-headed screws (this allows extra)
✔ Nails: 50 x 25 mm-long flat-headed nails (this allows extra)
✔ Soft galvanized wire: 600 mm

Exploded view of the former for the Roman arch shrine

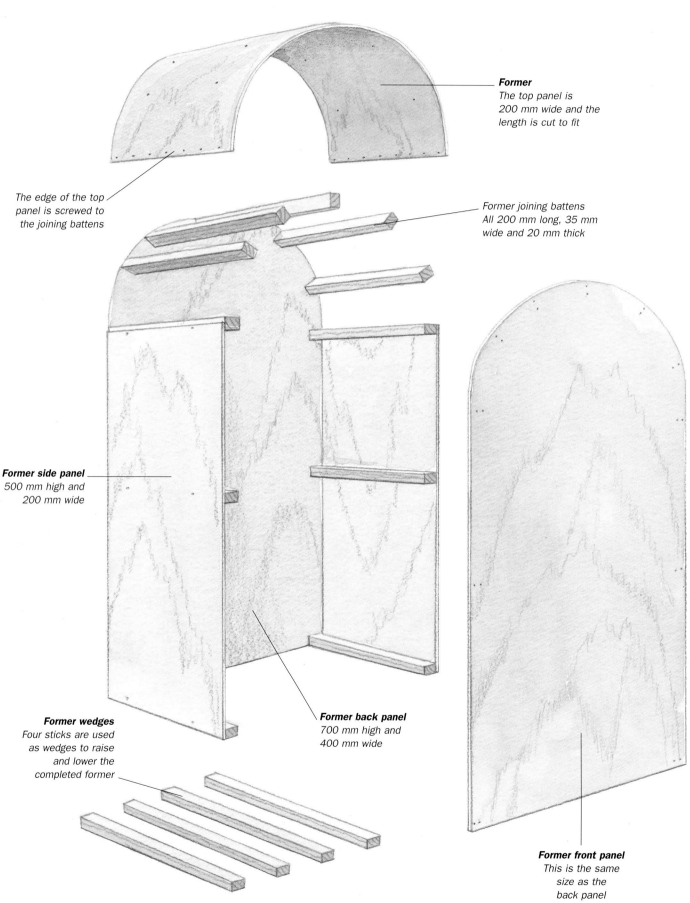

Former
The top panel is 200 mm wide and the length is cut to fit

The edge of the top panel is screwed to the joining battens

Former joining battens
All 200 mm long, 35 mm wide and 20 mm thick

Former side panel
500 mm high and 200 mm wide

Former wedges
Four sticks are used as wedges to raise and lower the completed former

Former back panel
700 mm high and 400 mm wide

Former front panel
This is the same size as the back panel

Exploded view of the Roman arch shrine

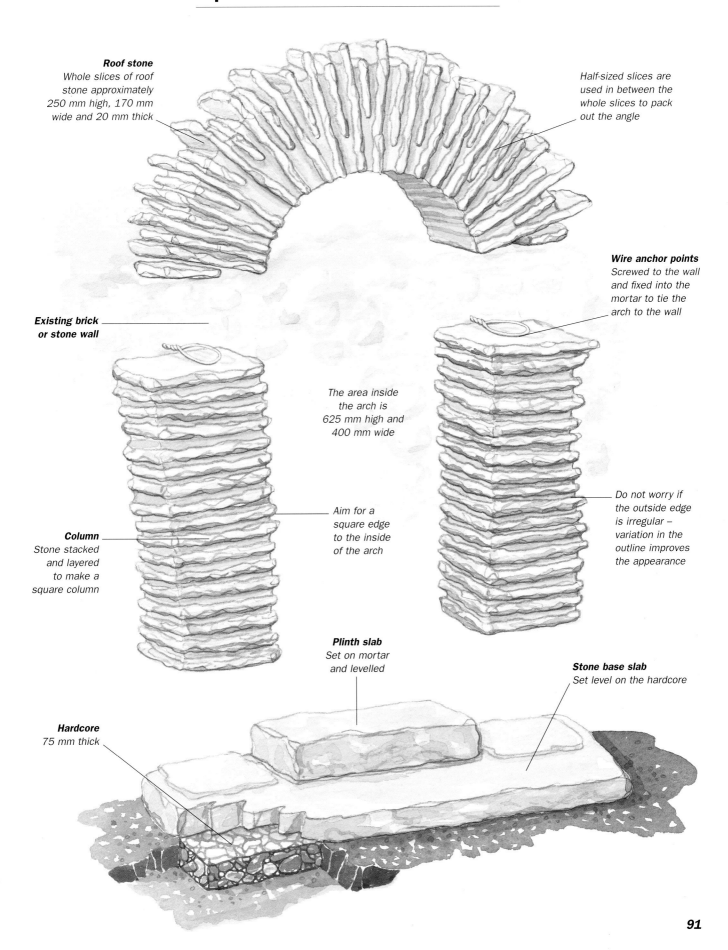

Roof stone
Whole slices of roof stone approximately 250 mm high, 170 mm wide and 20 mm thick

Half-sized slices are used in between the whole slices to pack out the angle

Existing brick or stone wall

Wire anchor points
Screwed to the wall and fixed into the mortar to tie the arch to the wall

The area inside the arch is 625 mm high and 400 mm wide

Aim for a square edge to the inside of the arch

Do not worry if the outside edge is irregular – variation in the outline improves the appearance

Column
Stone stacked and layered to make a square column

Plinth slab
Set on mortar and levelled

Stone base slab
Set level on the hardcore

Hardcore
75 mm thick

Making the Roman arch shrine

2 Covering the former
Cover the sides of the former with plywood. Ease the plywood over the curve and screw it to the joining battens. Use a generous quantity of screws.

1 Making the former
Build the front and back of the former with the two sheets of plywood, setting them 200 mm apart, as shown in the working drawing. Nail or screw the plywood shapes directly to the ends of the 200 mm-long joining battens.

3 Laying the base slab
Clear and level the site and compact the earth with the sledgehammer. Lay a 75 mm layer of hardcore and compact it with the sledgehammer. Set the base slab in place on generous blobs of mortar. Make checks with the spirit level.

4 Setting up the plinth slab
Bed the plinth slab in mortar on the base slab. Use the tape measure and spirit level to ensure that it is levelled and centred on the base slab.

5 Positioning the former

Place wedges of wood on the plinth and set the former on top of it, hard against the wall. Make sure that it is levelled and centred. Pay particular attention to the side-on view, making sure that the former is not tilting forwards (it can tilt backwards slightly).

6 Building the arch

Mix the mortar to a butter-smooth consistency and start to build layers of stone on each side of the former to make the square columns. Ensure that the stacks are both vertically and horizontally level, by making regular checks with the spirit level.

7 Anchor wires

Screw twists of wire to the wall at four or five places around the top of the arch, to provide anchor points for the stonework. As you build up the columns, insert the ends of the wire into the mortar between the slices of stone, to help hold the structure firm.

8 Forming the arch

Stack pieces of stone over the curved top of the former, setting half-slices between them to ensure a good spacing. Finally, when the mortar is dry and hard, use the pointing trowel to sculpt the mortar to reveal the edges of the stone.

Glossary

Back-filling
Filling a space that exists around a foundation or wall with earth.

Bedding
The process of setting (and levelling) a stone in a bed or layer of wet mortar.

Buttering
Using a trowel to spread a piece of stone with wet mortar, just prior to setting it in position, for example in a wall.

Compacting
Using a hammer or roller to squash down a layer of sand, earth or hardcore.

Coursing
Bedding a number of stones in mortar in order to build a horizontal course.

Curing time
The time taken for mortar or concrete to become firm and stable. "Part cured" means that the mortar or concrete is solid enough to continue work.

Dressing
Using a hammer, chisel or trowel to trim a stone to size; alternatively to create a textured finish on its surface.

Floating
Using a metal, plastic or wooden float to skim wet concrete or mortar to a smooth and level finish.

Levelling
Using a spirit level to confirm whether or not a structure or stone is level, and then going on to make adjustments to bring individual stones into line.

Marking out
Using string, pegs and a tape measure to set out the size of a foundation on the ground. Also to mark out an individual stone in readiness for cutting.

Planning
The whole procedure of considering a project, viewing the site, making drawings, and working out amounts and costs, prior to actually starting work.

Pointing
Using a trowel or a tool of your choice to fill, shape and texture mortar joints.

Raking out
Using a trowel to rake out some mortar in a joint in order that the edges of a stone are more clearly revealed.

Sighting
To judge by eye, or to look down or along a wall, in order to determine whether or not a structure is level.

Siting
Making decisions as to where – in the garden or on the plot – a structure is going to be positioned.

Sourcing
The process of questioning suppliers by phone, visit, letter or e-mail, in order to ascertain the best source for materials.

Tamping
Using a length of wood to compact and level wet concrete.

Trial run
Running through the procedure of setting out the components of a structure without using concrete or mortar, or trying a technique, in order to find out whether it will be successful.

Trimming
Using a hammer, chisel, the edge of large trowel, or a tool of your own choosing to bring the edge of a piece of stone to a good finish. It is very similar to Dressing (see opposite).

Watering or damping
Wetting a stone before bedding in on mortar, to prevent the stone sucking the water out of the mortar.

Wedging
Using small pieces of stone to wedge larger pieces of stone so that they reach a desired level.

Wire brushing
Using a wire-bristled brush to remove dry mortar from the face of a stone.

Suppliers

UK

Consult the telephone directory for details of your local garden centre, builders' yard or stone merchant.

The Brick Warehouse
18–22 Northdown Street
London N1 9BG
Tel: (020) 7833 9992
(Brick and stone products)

Buffalo Granite
(UK) Ltd
The Vestry
St Clement's Church
Treadgold Street
London W11 4BP
Tel: (020) 7221 7930
(Stone merchant)

The Natural Stone Co.
Elm Cottage
Ockham Road
North Ockham
Woking, Surrey
GU23 6NW
Tel: (01483) 211311
(Natural stone merchant)

Pinks Hill Landscape
Merchants
Off Broad Street
Wood Street Village
Guildford
Surrey GU3 3BP
Tel: 01483 571620
(Large range of natural and reproduction stone products, including feature stones, boulders, flags, rockery and walling stone, Japanese lanterns and statues)

Tarmac TopPave Ltd
Head Office: Wergs Hall
Wergs Hall Road
Wolverhampton
Staffordshire
WV8 2HZ
Tel: (01902) 774052
www.toppave.co.uk
General enquiries and details of stockists:
(08702) 413450
(Block pavers, decorative pavers, kerbing and edging blocks)

The York Handmade
Brick Co. Ltd
Forest Lane, Alne
York YO61 1TU
Tel: (01347) 838881
Fax: (01347) 838885
www.yorkhandmade.co.uk
Southern sales office:
(01909) 540680
(Handmade bricks, pavers and terracotta floor tiles)

General DIY/ garden stores (outlets nationwide, phone for details of nearest branch)

B & Q plc
Head Office:
Portswood House
1 Hampshire
Corporate Park
Chandlers Ford
Eastleigh
Hampshire SO53 3YX
Tel: (01703) 256256

Focus Do-It-All
Group Ltd
Head Office:
Gawsworth House
Westmere Drive, Crewe
Cheshire CW1 6XB
Tel: (01384) 456456

Homebase Ltd
Beddington House
Railway Approach
Wallington
Surrey SM6 0HB
Tel: (020) 8784 7200
www.homebase.co.uk

Wickes
Wickes House
120–138 Station Road
Harrow, Middlesex
HA1 2QB
Tel: (0870) 6089001
www.wickes.co.uk

AUSTRALIA

ABC Timber &
Building Supplies
Pty Ltd
46 Auburn Road
Regents Park,
NSW 2143
Tel: (02) 9645 2511

BBC Hardware
Head Office: Bld. A
Cnr. Cambridge and
Chester Streets
Epping, NSW 2121
Tel: (02) 9876 0888

Bowens Timber and
Building Supplies
135–173 Macaulay Road
North Melbourne
VIC 3051
Tel: (03) 9328 1041

Bunnings Building
Supplies
Head Office:
152 Pilbara Street
Welshpool, WA 6106
Tel: (08) 9365 1555

Pine Rivers
Landscaping
Supplies
93 South Pine Road
Strathpine, QLD 4500
Tel: (07) 3205 6708

Sydney Stone Yard
1/3A Stanley Road
Randwick, NSW 2031
Tel: (02) 9326 4479

Sydney Stone Company
Mona Vale Road
Mona Vale, NSW 2103
Tel: (02) 9979 9458
(Sandstone and bluestone)

Melocco Pty Ltd
849 Princes Highway
Springvale, VIC 3171
Tel: (03) 9546 0211
www.melocco.com.au
(Sandstone, granite, bluestone)

Gosford Quarries
300 Johnston Street
Annandale, NSW 2038
Tel: (02) 9810 7555
www.gosfordquarries.com.au
(Sandstone and granite)

International Sandstone
and Granite
11 Old Pacific Highway
Yatala, QLD 4207
Tel: (07) 3383 6999
www.isandstone.com.au

NEW ZEALAND

Firth Industries
Branches nationwide
Freephone: 0800 800 576
(Masonry)

Placemakers
Branches nationwide
Freephone:
0800 425 2269
(Masonry)

Stevenson Building
Supplies
(Branches throughout
Auckland)
Freephone: 0800 610 710
(Blocks, bricks, paving, concrete)

Southtile
654 North Road
Invercargill
Tel: (03) 215 9179
Fax: (03) 215 7178
Freephone: 0800 768 848
www.southtile.co.nz
(Tiles and bricks)

Index

AG&G Books would like to
thank Garden and Wildlife
Matters Photographic Library
for contributing the photographs
used on pages 7 and 18-23.